Lynda Field is a trained counsello~~~~~~~~~~~
who specialises in personal and group development. She is
the author of thirteen titles, including the best-selling
Weekend Life Coach, *60 Ways to Feel Amazing* and *60
Ways to Change Your Life*. In addition to giving seminars
and workshops, she runs a telephone and on-line coaching
service, and writes articles for a variety of national
magazines. She lives in Essex, UK.

Visit Lynda on-line at www.weekendlifecoach.com

By the same author

365 Inspirations for a Great Life

60 Ways to Change Your Life

60 Ways to Feel Amazing

The Little Book of Woman Power

60 Tips for Self-Esteem

Creating Self-Esteem

60 Ways to Heal Your Life

More than 60 Ways to Make Your Life Amazing

Self-Esteem for Women

The Self-Esteem Workbook

Just Do It Now!

Be Yourself

Weekend Life Coach

Weekend Love Coach

How to get the love you want in 48 hours

Lynda Field

Vermilion
LONDON

1 3 5 7 9 10 8 6 4 2

First published in 2005 by Vermilion,
an imprint of Ebury Press, Random House,
20 Vauxhall Bridge Road, London SW1V 2SA

Random House Australia (Pty) Limited
20 Alfred Street, Milsons Point, Sydney,
New South Wales 2061, Australia

Random House New Zealand Limited
18 Poland Road, Glenfield,
Auckland 10, New Zealand

Random House South Africa (Pty) Limited
Endulini, 5A Jubilee Road,
Parktown 2193, South Africa

The Random House Group Limited Reg. No. 954009
Papers used by Vermilion are natural, recyclable products
made from wood grown in sustainable forests.

Typeset by SX Composing DTP, Rayleigh, Essex
Printed and bound in Great Britain by
Bookmarque Ltd, Croydon, Surrey

A CIP catalogue record for this book is available from
the British Library

ISBN 0-09190238-X

Contents

To Sue Roberts, great friend and confidante.
Thanks for the title!

Acknowledgements

THANK YOU TO:

My husband Richard, who is the love of my life.

My children, Leilah, Jack and Alex, who are my pride and joy.

Alaska, my granddaughter, who is full of fun and love.

My parents Barbara and Idwal Goronwy, whose relationship is an inspiration.

My mother-in-law, Mary Field, who is always enthusiastic and go-getting.

The rest of my fabulous family, whose love and support make everything possible.

Barbara Higham, who is always there for me.

All my clients and colleagues, who keep me on my toes and remind me of what is important.

The wonderful team at Ebury, who have supported me all the way. With special thanks to my brilliant editor, Judith Kendra, who is always full of new creative ideas and to Caroline Newbury for her focus, clarity and friendship.

Preface
Turn Your Hopes
into Reality

*There are times when life surprises one, and
anything may happen, even what one had
hoped for.*

The clients of life coaches are usually realistic people who
know that they have the power to change the course of
their lives and are ready to do whatever it takes to get the
life they want. But over the years I have noticed that
whenever we venture into discussing their love relationships, even the most level-headed of them can lose the
plot and begin to drift into a haze of uncertainty and
romantic fantasies.

Yes, life can certainly surprise us with amazing gifts,
even with the thing that we most hoped for; but then
again it might not! We cannot afford to wait for that
enchanted evening when we will see a stranger across a
crowded room and *know* that *he is the one*. And we don't
have to leave it to fate or circumstance to deliver a
fabulous relationship to our door, because we can take

charge of getting the love we want and we can start right now.

If you feel that you need to get to grips with your love life, you are certainly not alone; more than 80 per cent of my clients have relationship issues to resolve. Whether they are struggling to enjoy their single status, looking to attract the right partner, attempting to rescue a failing relationship, recovering from a break-up, working out whether their partnership is worth saving or facing other dilemmas of the heart, I am always able to tell them that their issues can be resolved.

If you are being tested by love at the moment, you will undoubtedly be struggling to find the clarity and the self-confidence you need in order to regain control of your emotions and your life. When your love life is in turmoil you will naturally feel confused for a while, but there is no reason for you to stay this way. Once you decide that you have had enough of heartache and misery or that you are just fed up with the lack of love in your life, you are ready and able to move forward. After more than 20 years of working as a life coach, counsellor and relationship expert, I can tell you that I know, without a doubt, that you have all that it takes to rise to your love challenge and to overcome it: you really can learn to attract the love you deserve.

As we go through the day, it's often hard enough just to keep track of the next task in hand, let alone to take the time to assess and reflect upon our intimate relationships. And yet this is exactly what we need to do if we want to be happy in love. You might think that you already spend an undue amount of time wondering, fretting and worrying about your relationships (or lack of them) but this sort of preoccupation never leads to a good resolution. You can spend the whole night talking to friends about what's wrong with your love life only to come away feeling as bad as, if not worse than, you did to start with. This is because you are focusing on your problems instead of your solutions. The more you talk about 'what's wrong', the worse you feel as you fall into a downward spiral of self-doubt and confusion.

A person who has been disappointed in love will often blame herself for her own 'inadequacies', which inevitably leads to a loss of confidence in her power to attract love, and so a vicious negative cycle begins. Or maybe she will blame her love interest, who turned out not to be the man she thought he was. Most of us will have experienced both these reactions and will know first-hand that neither of these two approaches turns us into a love goddess!

The answer is to take the winning strategies of life coaching and to apply them to your love issues – you just need love coaching! *Weekend Love Coach* shows you how to get smart about how relationships really work. Why do you think that some people seem to have everything going for them? How can they be so positive and brimming with enthusiasm *as well as* having brilliant relationships? Did these people just get lucky in love as well as in everything else? Let me tell you this: these people are no different from you; they have no special tricks up their sleeve, they just decided that they deserved the very best that life (and love) could offer and they got clear about their goals and then they went for them!

Weekend Love Coach offers you the chance to get your love life in order once and for all! Allocate some time to spend alone relaxing with this book and focusing on you and your needs. Put yourself first next weekend and have a 48-hour personal love coaching session. I know that you have what it takes to make a real go of this and come out brimming with confidence and the ability to go for exactly what you want in your relationships. You never need settle for anything less than the best; you deserve to be respected, supported, nurtured and loved – *this is your goal!*

Introduction
Get the Love You Want

. . . it doesn't surprise me one bit that Viagra for women won't work. All a woman needs is for a gorgeous man to fall head over heels in love with her. Unfortunately, that's something that can't be bought over the counter.

INGRID TARRANT (WIFE OF TV STAR
CHRIS TARRANT)

Pfizer, the company behind Viagra, has given up its attempt to produce a female version of the sex pill. At the end of an eight-year research project involving 3,000 women, the team at Pfizer have concluded that men and women are not sexually aroused in the same way. The scientists have deduced that while a man's arousal can be a purely physical response, a woman's is triggered by emotional factors. Yes, I know you knew that already! Apparently Pfizer is now searching for a drug that will alter a woman's brain chemistry. But of course this amazing aphrodisiac is already available; we call it love, and although it can't be bought over the counter, we can find out exactly how to get it.

It may surprise you to know that the principles of life coaching can be applied to your love relationships just as effectively as to any other area of your life. We find this hard to believe because we are inclined to imagine that love and romance are mysterious forces that hover in some fabulous esoteric realm somewhere beyond our reach and control. But if we hang on to such fanciful images, love will remain a remote ideal and an impossible dream and we will never be able to make it a real part of our life. This book is full of practical tips and strategies to show you how to bring love into your life and how to keep it at the heart of your relationships.

When we are feeling great, the world is a wonderful place and anything feels possible. Hope, appreciation and happiness bubble up from inside us and every day brings new opportunities. It's so simple: when we love our life, our life loves us back; when we radiate love, we attract it! Your thoughts, beliefs and feelings about yourself and your life create an aura that you carry with you everywhere you go. Others are automatically attracted or repelled by this invisible energy; they can sense it at the very deepest level. Someone once said, 'People and situations walk through the doors of our expectations.' Think about who and what you have invited into your life through your own doors.

Weekend Love Coach takes a strategic approach to getting the love you want. It looks closely at the energy you are putting out and shows you exactly how to step into the skin of that confident and charismatic woman who is longing to emerge. Face it: you are no longer willing to put up with second best in your life, and that includes your love life! You want to feel positive, upbeat and emotionally fulfilled, and you are determined to get what you want; that is why you bought this book.

Women want to be turned on mentally and emotionally as well as sexually. We want the works: attention, romance, stability, candlelit dinners, and thoughtful and passionate sex. We want a man who can listen to us without trying to 'fix' us – and he also needs to be able to change nappies, do the Tesco run and know how to use a vacuum cleaner. Why would we settle for anything less than a man who can give us what we need?

But sometimes we do. When we are high on the exhilaration of a new romance, our judgement can become clouded, and when we eventually take off those rose-tinted specs we realise that he wasn't the man we thought (hoped) that he was. You are not the only one to go down this route; we have all been there, and some of us have been there too many times to count! I consider all 'failed' relationships to be part of an important love learning curve. Making mistakes is the way we learn what doesn't work. This book will show you how to learn from your mistakes and move on. You don't have to keep falling for the 'wrong' type. Loving a man does not mean sacrificing yourself; if it hurts, it isn't love.

The idea to write this book came from you, my clients and my readers. Many hundreds of you contacted me after reading *Weekend Life Coach*, and I felt inspired by the ways you had used the principles in the book to help you to make huge changes in your life. As relationship issues tend to be high on the list for life coaching clients, I began to think about creating my own love coaching programme. Soon I was using these new techniques and strategies with clients and workshop participants and almost before I knew it the ideas for *Weekend Love Coach* had emerged.

How to use *Weekend Love Coach*

You will need to find some peaceful time to work through this book. If time is tight, then schedule it in your diary. For those of you who can take a weekend to concentrate on your love life, I can promise you the rewards will be well worth it. Over the years I have discovered that an easy, calm approach to coaching always brings the most dramatic and long-lasting changes. *Weekend Love Coach* offers a relaxed and focused method for taking control of your love life. All you have to do is to find a peaceful environment where you can let go of your everyday preoccupations and concentrate solely on yourself and your needs. So kick off your shoes and get ready to indulge yourself in some quality 'me' time.

I suggest that you buy an attractive spiral-bound notebook that you can use to record your thoughts, feelings and reflections as you work through the book. Search for the most beautiful notebook you can find. After all, this is your love journal! Let your love coaching weekend be a thoroughly cleansing and liberating experience. We will be looking for solutions and not dwelling on problems. Certainly emotions will arise and there will be issues to be dealt with, but all the while I will be offering my support and encouragement. There are Instant Tips throughout the book to help you stay upbeat and focused. And at the end of each chapter you will find a Meditation Moment, designed to keep you feeling relaxed and centred.

Part One of this book is an easy guide to taking control of your love life and I take you through a number of steps to show you how to do this.

Step 1: Know What You Want reveals that the quality of your love relationship is an exact reflection of your personal levels of self-confidence. When you are brimming with self-belief and optimism, you expect the very best of yourself and of everyone else and so you attract positive and supportive relationships. You have the power to get the love you want. In this step I show you how you can learn to become a winner and achieve your dreams in life and love.

Step 2: Become a Love Magnet shows you how to draw love into your life with your powerful, upbeat personal magnetism. Self-confidence leads directly to relationship confidence. When you radiate positivity and love, you become irresistibly fascinating to everyone you meet! So what are you waiting for?

Step 3: Find Romance and get that fabulously heady feeling of falling in love. Check out your relationship prospects and discover exactly how he scores on the attraction stakes. Learn how to take positive action and create your own personal action plan to clarify and achieve your love goals; you *can* find true romance!

Step 4: Take Charge of Your Love Life explains very clearly why many relationships fail. Without relationship self-esteem your love life is doomed, so find out if you are acting like a love magnet or behaving like a love victim. Learn how to be assertive in your love interactions and the quality of your intimate relationships will improve beyond your wildest dreams. You deserve a gorgeous, fabulous man so make sure you get one!

Step 5: Be a Sex Goddess reminds you that you are a girl who loves her own sexuality and knows how she gets turned on (and off). Become super-body-confident and get out there and show off your own original and remarkable self. Tap into your natural sexiness and feel and look your amazing best. When you can release your inner sex goddess, your libido will soar and, yes, you will be hot!

Step 6: Get Him Talking invites you to make your relationship close and loving. He is not like you; he thinks, feels and expresses himself differently. Find out how he ticks and why he can't listen very well. Discover how and why the sexes behave differently, and take your love life to a fantastic new level of intimacy.

Step 7: Flirt Your Way to Success shows you how to have fun while also making others feel good about themselves. Natural flirts are high in self-belief and body confidence and they know exactly how to bring out the best in others. Learn to become a natural flirt and bring a sparkle to your life (and your love life).

Let these seven steps guide you whenever you feel that your love life has gone awry. Don't let yourself be dragged down into an emotional pit that seems to offer no way out. There is always a way to resolve your love issues, even at times when this seems very hard to believe. The first thing to do is check that you are keeping to your guidelines. Are you taking all of the seven steps? Find out by asking yourself the following questions:

- Am I clear about what I want? Do I believe in myself?
- Am I radiating love and positivity?
- Is my love action plan in place? Am I focused on my goals?
- Am I acting like a love magnet or behaving like a victim?
- Are my sexual needs being met?
- Are we talking to each other or has there been a communication breakdown?
- Am I using my flirting skills to my best advantage?

When you use the simple tips and tools in Part One, you will start to become your very own love coach. Who knows you and your needs better than you do? There are as many ways to love and be loved as there are people on the planet. No one way is the right way for everyone, but you can be sure that one way is right for you. Discover your love needs and get in touch with your feminine charms. You can find happiness and fun in a romantic relationship and still keep the excitement alive if it turns into a long-term commitment. You have what it takes to create the love life of your dreams. Just believe this and start creating.

Part Two shows you how to become a winner in the game of love by getting to understand how your own love relationships really work.

What positive qualities do you bring with you to your relationships? Can you trust your instincts and do you follow them? Do you love and respect yourself or are you looking for a man to give you self-confidence and a feeling of value? Have you ever compromised your integrity and self-respect in order to catch or keep a man? *Weekend Love Coach* shows you how to be strong, confident and self-assured. A woman who recognises her own worth is charismatic and sexy; self-confidence is the greatest aphrodisiac of all.

And how do you know for sure if he is the one? If you have ever been in a situation where you are uncertain whether to stay in or leave a relationship, you will have asked yourself this question. We will put your relationship under the microscope so that you can assess it realistically and then make your decision.

Maybe you are trying to get him to commit. This can be

tricky. First of all you need to check your own commitment levels; how serious are you, really? And if you are sure that 'this is it', then use your knowledge and understanding of the way he works to get your result. We know how men love to feel that they are travelling light along the highway of life; but, hey, we can show them that our baggage is stylish and feather-weight.

And if you are nursing a broken heart, then you need lots of nurturing, attention and support. Heartbreak is painful but not terminal. Right now you may be feeling that you will never recover, but you will, I promise. The way forward lies in understanding how grief works (you are grieving a loss here). With tips and strategies to help you let go of the pain, it won't be long before you stop describing yourself as heartbroken and start telling friends that you are between boyfriends!

Read *Weekend Love Coach* and do the exercises and meditations. Try the tips and suggestions and just watch how you change. Love, romance and practicality do go together. Don't think that you will lose the romance if you understand what is going on between you; the opposite is true. Know yourself and know your lover and turn your relationship into one that is open, trusting, caring and understanding. There is nothing quite as sexy and romantic as this!

Part One

SEVEN STEPS TO BEING YOUR OWN LOVE COACH

STEP 1
KNOW WHAT YOU WANT

STEP 2
BECOME A LOVE MAGNET

STEP 3
FIND ROMANCE

STEP 4
TAKE CHARGE OF YOUR LOVE LIFE

STEP 5
BE A SEX GODDESS

STEP 6
GET HIM TALKING

STEP 7
FLIRT YOUR WAY TO SUCCESS

7 STEPS TO BEING YOUR OWN LOVE COACH

Step 1
Know What You Want

Life will work for me when I realise . . . I have the power to walk right! The power to talk right! And the power to live right!

IYANLA VANZANT

And love will work for you when you realise that you have the power to love right!

When their relationships disintegrate, women usually think that it's their fault, asking themselves, 'What did I do wrong?' and 'How can I make it better?' So many of my (female) clients are full of self-criticism and guilt when their love lives fall apart, and you too may have been down this rocky road. We are highly likely to take all the blame, thinking that if only we could love 'right' he might stay, change, love us, be the man we know he can be . . .

It takes two to make a success of a relationship; it takes two people who are committed to each other because they both feel that their needs are being met. Loving right always means getting yourself straight first. The most important relationship you ever have is the one you have

| 13

with yourself; get this right and all your other relationships will come together. When you are self-confident and know what you want from life and love, you will no longer be prepared to compromise yourself and your dreams, and you will not look for your security in someone else. If being with a man means you can't be true to yourself, then he is not right for you. And if you ever find yourself holding back and not following your true direction because you are protecting his feelings, then you are definitely not loving right!

Marie, 23, was a successful model whose work took her to exotic locations all around the world. She earned a lot of money and had a glamorous lifestyle, but in spite of this she was always doubting herself and looking for others to take charge and to tell her what to do. Ryan, her long-term boyfriend, was jealous and controlling; he was constantly imagining that she was having affairs and rang her continually when she was away on location. Although this sometimes got a bit much, Marie loved being the focus of all his attention. When she came home after a few weeks' work in Australia, Ryan told her that he had been lost without her and he demanded that she stopped her regular nights out with her girlfriends. He said he loved her too much to share her with anyone, and she felt flattered and agreed to go out only with him. But soon she was feeling trapped by his attentiveness and was too scared to tell him. Then, after a romantic night out, he asked her to marry him but said he could only make that commitment if she finally stopped modelling. She thought that his inability to let her have a life of her own meant that he must truly love her and so she agreed to give up her career. Six months after their fairytale wedding, Ryan left her (he said he was feeling bored and stifled) to take up with an actress who was just starting to make a name for herself on TV.

At first Marie was heartbroken. She picked up with her girlfriends again and got her life together but she was never able to get back into the modelling scene. It took some weeks of coaching before Marie felt strong enough to accept that the failure of her marriage was not her fault. Next she felt angry with Ryan for ruining her career and running out on her. And then, as she worked on her confidence levels, she began to understand the role that she had played in this sad story. In the end she realised that they had both suffered from low self-confidence. Their personal insecurities and lack of clarity about what

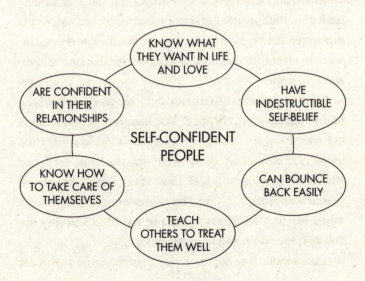

KNOW WHAT THEY WANT IN LIFE AND LOVE

ARE CONFIDENT IN THEIR RELATIONSHIPS

HAVE INDESTRUCTIBLE SELF-BELIEF

SELF-CONFIDENT PEOPLE

KNOW HOW TO TAKE CARE OF THEMSELVES

CAN BOUNCE BACK EASILY

TEACH OTHERS TO TREAT THEM WELL

they really wanted were problems which their relationship could never have solved. Marie then knew that she could never feel secure in a relationship until she became more self-confident. Loving right would have meant not putting Ryan's needs before her own.

Believe and Win

You have the power to get whatever you want from life: happiness, success, love . . . all these can be yours. Look around at the winners who reach for their dreams and ask yourself: What makes them different? How do they stand out? What qualities do they have? It's easy to think that some people are just born lucky, but the truth is that anyone who has achieved anything worthwhile has had to work for it. Self-doubt is a demon that we all have to conquer, and when we decide to get out there and really go for something, of course we run the risk of failure. It is our inner strength (or lack of it) that makes or breaks us; we can either be our own biggest supporter or our own sternest critic.

What is the most frightening: to try to do something and to fail or not to try at all? The happiest people I come across are always those who are ready to have a go. Then even if things don't quite turn out the way they had planned, they can still feel good about their upbeat and positive approach to life. The go-getters are always life's winners. They are ready to try and try again and they are full of hope and positive expectations.

The minute you decide to try something new you are

filled with fresh excitement and enthusiasm; let this powerful energy propel you forward towards your new goal. Don't be deterred by the obstacles along the way. Know that you have all that it takes to overcome them. Self-confident people have indestructible self-belief. *Nothing* can take away their feeling of self-worth, and they bounce back again and again. You can feel like this. You too have all that it takes to go for what you want and to ride the ups and downs that life inevitably brings. No one has a smooth trip, but just think how you will feel if you don't even give yourself a chance to get out there and give things a try!

J.K. Rowling says, 'I am an extraordinarily lucky person, doing what I love best in the world. I'm sure that I will always be a writer. It was wonderful enough just to be published.' Rather like her books' hero, Harry Potter, J.K. Rowling's life has a magical feel about it. However, her rise to fame is not part of a fairytale but the result of hard work in the face of overwhelming odds. With a failed marriage behind her and a baby daughter to support, the unemployed Rowling wrote *Harry Potter and the Philosopher's Stone* during a very unhappy period of her life. All the major publishers turned down her manuscript, but eventually Bloomsbury Press accepted it, and the rest, of course, is history. Now Joanne has remarried and has another child, and another on the way, and Harry Potter has become a worldwide phenomenon.

Do you think that J.K. Rowling struggled to write that first book? Of course she did. It actually took her five years to complete. But she kept going and believed in herself and didn't give up. There is magic in self-belief. Try it!

INSTANT TIP

SEEK YOUR OWN OPINION

When you face a tricky problem where do you turn? Supportive friends are a good source of useful feedback and advice, but the final decisions must always rest with you. If you are high in self-belief, then you will trust your own thoughts and feelings and will be able to follow through with appropriate action.

A person with self-belief:

- Never compares herself with others.
- Knows that she is her own woman and that nobody else can understand her as well as she can.
- Listens to helpful advice and comments but never blindly follows others' opinions.
- Trusts her instincts and listens to her heart.
- Recognises that she will make mistakes and learns from them and moves on.
- Depends upon her own judgement and always gives herself time to work things through.
- Values rest and relaxation as much as action-planning and activity.
- Knows that when she is calm and focused she will make the best decisions.

- ACCEPTS THAT THERE WILL BE DAYS WHEN HER SELF-BELIEF IS NOT SO STRONG AND WILL WAIT UNTIL SHE IS FEELING MORE POSITIVE BEFORE COMMITTING HERSELF TO ANY COURSE OF ACTION.

We teach other people how to treat us

Putting our own needs first does not come naturally to most women. We are natural carers, nurturers and forgivers; it's in our hormones! Now these are great qualities, but unless they are carefully balanced by rationality, logic and self-preservation, we can find ourselves in big trouble. Just like Marie, we may easily sell ourselves short.

Have you noticed how women who are on their own and obviously enjoying their single status are like man magnets? It seems that guys can't stay away from women who have got a life that doesn't depend on them. We are all attracted to the energy that confidence creates; there is no one quite as fascinating as the person who is self-reliant and at ease with themselves.

We teach other people how to treat us. If we respect ourselves, then the people we meet will respond to this and treat us well. And if we have low self-belief and can't trust our own judgement, then naturally others will pick up on our doubts and believe them to be true. When our confidence has taken a knock we feel insecure, and this shows. The relationships we attract when we are feeling bad are likely to reflect our low self-opinion and in this state we are more inclined to put up with poor behaviour from others. But when we are brimming with self-belief and optimism we expect the best of ourselves and of everyone else and so we attract positive and supportive relationships. What are you teaching others about how you deserve to be treated? Try the self-confidence test below and find out what people are picking up from your thoughts, feelings and behaviour.

EXERCISE:

The self-confidence test

Read each of the following statements and ask yourself if they are true for you. Score as follows:

1 almost never
2 sometimes
3 often
4 almost always

1 I believe in myself.
2 I know what I want.
3 I find it easy to go for my goals.
4 I am a person who can make things happen.
5 It's easy for me to express my feelings.
6 I can accept my mistakes and move on.
7 I am relaxed in social situations.

8 My happiness does not depend on the behaviour of others.

9 I don't act like a victim.

10 I can accept that I can't please everyone.

If you scored 10–19

You are not at your best right now. It can be hard for you to get the most from life because indecision and lack of focus are holding you back. Consider each of these statements again and think about your answers. When is your self-confidence challenged most? How could you bring more positive and assertive energy into your life? What one thing could you do that would give you more self-confidence? Do it!

If you scored 20–29

Your confidence is often evident, but there are still some situations where you find it hard to be sure of yourself. You know when your self-doubts start to creep in and you would like to be able to overcome them. Sometimes you are worried about what other people are thinking and this stops you saying what's on your mind. Look at your answers again. What are those self-limiting beliefs that are holding you back? Why are you believing less than the best about yourself? Let your positive self shine through!

If you scored 30–40

You are self-confident and you know that the way to stay like this is to maintain a positive outlook and trust yourself and your judgements. You know how to say no without feeling guilty and you have developed some strategies that allow you to keep upbeat even when the going gets rough. Your high score reflects your levels of self-confidence. Others treat you with the respect you rightly deserve.

Get a life and then get a man

If you think about any couple you know who are happy together, you will probably notice that they each have their own individual aspirations and interests. The trick is to get a life and *then* get a love life. When we go into a relationship looking for someone to fill an empty space inside us, the chances are that this won't work. We can't expect another person to make our life feel worthwhile, and if we try to do this, the partnership can never be equal and mutually supporting.

So before you look for a man, look at your life! Decide to be your best in all that you do; reach for your potential and go for your dreams. Take charge of yourself: face any obstacles and decide to overcome them. You are an amazing woman and you deserve to give yourself the very best chance. Your time is now. Take whatever steps you need to create the life that you want.

Lauren, 33, is in publishing and loves her job. She has had two long-term relationships but has now decided to take care of herself and her own needs before she even thinks about getting serious with a man. She says, 'I have spent a good few years taking the back seat so that I could be an

INSTANT TIP

TAKE CARE OF YOURSELF

SELF-CONFIDENCE IS A GIFT THAT YOU WILL RECEIVE AS SOON AS YOU START TO TAKE YOURSELF SERIOUSLY. THIS MEANS PUTTING YOURSELF FIRST INSTEAD OF LAST AND ALWAYS REMEMBERING THAT YOU NEED TO KEEP YOURSELF TOGETHER IF YOU ARE GOING TO BE OF ANY USE TO OTHERS. IF THE IDEA OF SELF-NURTURING MAKES YOU FEEL UNCOMFORTABLE, IT'S TIME TO ASK YOURSELF WHY.

- START TO CARE FOR YOURSELF IN EXACTLY THE WAY THAT YOU WOULD CARE FOR A LOVED ONE.
- GIVE YOURSELF A BREAK; LET YOURSELF OFF THE HOOK (OR HOOKS!).
- SPEND SOME QUALITY TIME ALONE, JUST HANGING OUT AND DOING WHAT YOU ENJOY MOST.
- LOOK AFTER YOURSELF: EAT WELL, SLEEP WELL AND EXERCISE WELL.
- SLOW DOWN AND APPRECIATE YOUR LIFE AND ALL YOU HAVE.
- KNOW THAT YOU ARE ALWAYS DOING YOUR BEST.
- FORGIVE YOURSELF.
- SMILE, EVEN IF YOU ARE ALONE, AND FEEL THOSE HAPPY HORMONES RUSHING THROUGH YOUR SYSTEM.
- REMEMBER THAT YOUR LIFE IS PRECIOUS – SAVOUR EACH MOMENT.

emotional support for the men in my life, but it didn't work because both times I ended up feeling resentful. Now I am going to enjoy my independence and develop my career and just be free to be myself without the pressure of trying to make a relationship work. I will only settle for an equal partnership now and I have no need or desire to be with a man who doesn't value me and my talents.' The irony is that now Lauren isn't looking at men they are all looking at her! Men are drawn to her confident and independent approach and they know that they will have to demonstrate positive qualities of their own if they are going to stand a chance with her. Self-confidence is sexy and it demands high standards of behaviour from others. Get your life sorted and become a self-confident woman who knows what she is worth and knows what she wants in life and in love.

Self-confidence leads to relationship confidence

You bring your whole self to every experience you have. Your thoughts, feelings and behaviour exist simultaneously; they are interrelated and affect each other. If your thoughts about yourself are validating and you believe that you are worthy, then you will feel positive about yourself and your behaviour will be confident and effective – you will be a person who makes things happen. Self-belief is at the very heart of self-confidence, and without it you will feel negative and insecure, which will lead to poor and ineffective behaviour.

Wherever you go you take yourself, and this is never so obvious as when you enter a relationship. Whatever the initial sexual chemistry between you, the quality of your relationship will depend entirely upon your levels of personal self-confidence. However much you fancy him, it will not work unless you **think, feel and act confidently**.

- When you **think confidently** you believe in yourself and trust your instincts. You know that you deserve to be treated with the utmost respect and you have a positive and optimistic approach to your relationship. You are open to changes and you think that you both have an equally important role in your partnership. You know what you want from the relationship.
- When you **feel confident** you have a strong sense of inner stability and security. You are in touch with your emotions and are not afraid to show your partner that you care. You love to give and receive spontaneous acts of affection and you expect to be appreciated.
- When you **act confidently** you are dependable and reliable and you can be decisive and effective. You are not afraid to take risks and you have good open communication skills. You expect your partner to be trustworthy and to share his thoughts and feelings with you.

A truly intimate relationship is one in which both partners have the confidence to be themselves and feel free to disclose their pain as well as their pleasure. If either partner is low in self-confidence, there will be communication and behavioural problems within the relationship, and it is unlikely to be a success.

Cast your mind back to any previous relationships that haven't worked out. Did you both enter the partnership with a healthy degree of self-confidence? If not, can you see how this lack was at the root of the problems that led to the breakdown of the relationship?

Ten instant self-confidence boosters

Our levels of self-confidence rise and fall. Sometimes when the going gets tough it's hard to reach inside ourselves and find the inner strength we need. If you are in a rut right now and your self-confidence is at a low ebb, look at the following checklist to see what you can do to bring some instant enthusiasm and vigour back into your life.

1   Put a smile on your face even if you don't feel like it. Fake it till you make it and before long you will be feeling better.
2   Look good! Treat yourself to a wonderful haircut, put on some make-up and step out there, girl!
3   Take a rest from your worries and go for a walk. You will be amazed at your changes in perception after you have 'walked out' your mood.
4   Let go of the need to be right all the time; you will feel surprisingly uplifted.
5   Create a new goal and take the first step towards it.

6 Respect your own needs and learn to say yes and no when you want to.

7 Get together with your most positive friends (the best tonic in the world!).

8 Repeat the mantra: 'I am a success!'

9 Take yourself out for the day to do something you love. Enjoy your own company and the pleasure of doing exactly what you want.

10 You are special and unique – don't forget this.

But how do you know if he's the right man for you?

So what exactly do you want from love? You might think this is an unusual question to ask, but then the first question in any coaching session is always, 'What do you want? Why have you come for coaching?' If you don't know what you want, how on earth can you set about getting it? Ah, but surely love is different. We can't pin it down and quantify it and we never know when it will appear. How can we apply a set of action-planning rules to the magical and elusive realms of romantic love?

Falling in love is a powerful and mysterious process. In the beginning every moment together is fabulously exciting and exhilarating, each kiss a mind-blowing experience, every touch ecstasy. No wonder we love to fall in love. But then, if this heady and enchanting experience leads to a long-term relationship, we come face to face with the daily reality of sharing our life with another person. And if you have ever been in a serious relationship you are bound to have found yourself at some stage asking the all-important question: 'Is he the right person for me?'

If you are asking yourself this question right now or if you are unattached and looking for the right relationship then love coaching offers a positive way forward. Those 'lucky' people you see who have a happy and loving partnership have not fallen on their feet by chance. When the whirl of romance turns into a relationship in which both partners are confident to share themselves in a wholehearted way, the prospects are very good. But this sort of open-hearted commitment does not just happen; it takes self-confidence, mutual consideration and dedication to the goals of the relationship.

I am speaking to you not just as a life coach and relationship expert but as a woman who has made some pretty poor relationship choices in the past. Sometimes the desire to be in love was all it took for me to get involved with a pair of sexy blue eyes and a cute butt. I never took the time to work out exactly what I wanted from a relationship and what sort of man would suit me. I think it's true that we probably spend more time choosing a new pair of shoes than we do in choosing a man.

Eventually, after a marriage breakdown, I was a single parent for a few years. Kids are great at exposing prospective love candidates who haven't got it in them to last the course! So, with men thin on the ground and my toddlers taking all my time, I lost all inclination to play the field – which was extremely fortunate for me, because when I forgot about men I found I got enthusiastic about my own life. I started a knitwear business and began running support groups for women. I had become a people pleaser in my relationship and now, on my own, I found my voice again.

By this time I was very happy alone and had no wish at all to get into a serious relationship. And then, when I had completely lost all my neediness, I met Richard. It was lust at first sight and then some emotional hard work before we both gave our relationship what it deserved. And yes we did (and do) live happily ever after.

I am sure that you, just like the rest of us, have made some wrong decisions in the love department, but all that is about to change. Your relationship choices are not like a lucky dip, although it may often feel like this. You *can* take control of your love life. Take heart and know that you do deserve to be loved.

MEDITATION MOMENT

FEEL THE LOVE INSIDE YOU

FIND A QUIET, COMFORTABLE PLACE AND RELAX. CLOSE YOUR EYES AND STEADY YOUR BREATHING AS YOU PREPARE YOURSELF TO LET GO OF ALL THE TENSION IN YOUR BODY AND IN YOUR MIND.

START WITH YOUR FEET AND, TAKING ONE AT A TIME, CONSCIOUSLY LET GO OF ANY STRESS AND PRESSURE. RELAX YOUR FEET. NOW RELAX YOUR LEGS,

---

AND THEN YOUR ABDOMEN AND ONWARDS UP THROUGH YOUR BODY, PAYING SPECIAL ATTENTION TO YOUR BACK, NECK, HEAD AND SHOULDER AREAS. WHEN YOUR WHOLE BODY FEELS RELAXED, ALLOW YOURSELF TIME TO ENJOY THIS FEELING OF LIGHTNESS.

NOW RELAX YOUR MIND BY IGNORING THE FLOW OF CONTINUAL THOUGHTS. EACH TIME YOU FIND YOURSELF THINKING, JUST LET THE THOUGHT GO AND CONCENTRATE ON YOUR BREATHING. AFTER A SHORT WHILE YOU WILL FEEL CALMER.

IMAGINE YOUR HEART, SEE ITS PERFECT SHAPE AND KNOW THAT IT IS FULL OF LOVE FOR YOU AND THE REST OF THE UNIVERSE. SURROUND YOUR HEART WITH A BEAUTIFUL PINK LIGHT; THIS IS THE LIGHT OF YOUR LOVE. FEEL THIS PINK LIGHT SURROUNDING YOU AND ENCASING YOU IN PURE LOVE. YES, LOVE IS INSIDE YOU. IMAGINE SENDING YOUR LOVING LIGHT OUT INTO THE WORLD. WHO DO YOU KNOW WHO COULD DO WITH SOME LOVE RIGHT NOW? BECOME AWARE OF YOUR FEELINGS AS YOU BROADCAST LOVE TO OTHERS. THE MORE LOVE YOU TRANSMIT, THE MORE LOVE YOU FEEL.

WHENEVER YOU FEEL TOUCHED BY LOVE, KNOW THAT THIS FEELING COMES FROM WITHIN YOU. NO ONE CAN 'GIVE YOU' LOVE; THEY CAN FEEL LOVING TOWARDS YOU, BUT UNLESS THERE IS ALREADY LOVE IN YOUR HEART YOU WON'T RECOGNISE IT. TOUCH THE LOVE INSIDE YOU; IT IS ALWAYS THERE JUST WAITING FOR YOU TO FEEL IT.

Step 2
Become a Love Magnet

I had a horrific childhood, and it's left me f***** up. Of all the things in life I want, I want to find love most. I've known some fantastic people, and I'm very lucky in that I have four amazing children – I'm grateful for that – but there's a hole in my life that can only be filled by love. I have been searching for it all my life, but it looks like I'm not very good at finding it.

JERRY HALL

Why is it that some people find themselves in loving successful partnerships while others (even the rich, talented and glamorous) struggle so hard to attract the love they seek? Are some of us really doomed to be unlucky in love, always searching for and never finding the perfect mate? Dr Richard Wiseman conducted a ten-year psychological study of more than 1,000 people. His exhaustive research led him to conclude that, 'People create much of their own good and bad luck through their thoughts, feelings and actions.' It seems that our beliefs create a self-fulfilling prophecy so that if you believe that you are lucky in love, then you are, and if you believe that you are not, then you are not! If you feel that you are in an unlucky cycle right now, ask yourself this question: 'Are you ready to get lucky in love?'

You attract the type of love that you think you deserve and you will only be truly appreciated, loved and supported when you can appreciate, love and support yourself. I know this is hard to swallow when you are feeling emotionally bruised and battered by a relationship, but it's true! Once you can accept that your love relationships reflect the love that you have for yourself, you have a fabulous and amazing tool. Self-confidence leads to relationship confidence: it all starts with you. Learn to radiate confidence, self-esteem and self-belief and you will become a love magnet rather than a love rat magnet!

EXERCISE:

Are you a love magnet?

Read the following statements.
Score **0** each time you answer **True**
Score **2** each time you answer **Untrue**

1 When I fall in love I often experience emotional pain.
2 I sometimes worry that my love partner may be losing interest in me.
3 I believe that I can change a man if I love him enough.
4 When I am in a relationship I don't always feel free to be myself.

5 I sometimes fall for the wrong type of man.

6 When a love relationship ends I often feel devastated.

7 I am unlucky in love.

8 I need to be in a relationship to feel complete.

9 I have never set any relationship goals; I just fall in love and see where it takes me.

10 I often put my partner's needs before my own.

If you scored 0–6

Your relationship history is poor and you have often felt let down in love. Look at each of your 'true' answers and consider how your thoughts, feelings or behaviour have directly affected the quality of your love life. You may often feel like a victim of love, but don't worry, you can change all this. As soon as you learn to project positive and assertive energy you will attract healthy love relationships.

If you scored 8–14

You are starting to become a love magnet, but there are still times when you attract poor behaviour in your relationships. Think about your 'untrue' answers; these demonstrate that you don't always lose your sense of self when you are in love. As you develop a stronger sense of who you are and how you expect to be treated, it will become easier and easier to get the love you want.

If you scored 16–20

Well done! You are definitely on your way to becoming a love magnet if you are not one already! Once you start to radiate self-belief and self-respect it has an amazing effect on your behaviour: you can trust your gut reactions, express your emotions and make good decisions in the love department. Although you might not be in a great relationship at the moment, you are happy with yourself, and this gives you the self-confidence that turns you into a love magnet.

If it hurts it isn't love

The gorgeous model and actress Jerry Hall has had her pick of rich and powerful men but at 48 has yet to find the love she desperately seeks. When she was 16 she left her childhood home in Texas (she describes her father as 'a violent man and a terrible father') and moved to Paris. She soon started living with Bryan Ferry and then met Mick Jagger when she was 19.

Jerry describes Mick as her soul mate as well as a good father and says, 'Mick is incredibly charming, talented, dynamic and funny, so it was easy to fall in love with him . . . Mick and I had this wonderful life together. It was just the infidelity that was too much . . . I really did think that I could change him. I thought he would settle down and be a wonderful partner, father and husband. But I had to give up.' Jerry describes her 25 years with Mick as a time of 'public humiliation and private heartbreak'. Eventually she had to accept that she couldn't change him and stop his pattern of serial infidelity.

I have yet to meet a woman who has never been seduced by the myth that she can change a man. And who among us can honestly say that she has never allowed herself to be treated badly? But once we have been there and done that, we can recognise the pattern of behaviour for what it is and decide not to go there again. The choice is always ours: to keep our self-respect and stand up for ourselves and what we deserve, or to lose every shred of self-esteem and to allow ourselves to become a victim of love. Jerry stayed and felt humiliated for a long time, and we can only begin to imagine what this did for her self-confidence. Describing her role in her marriage she said, 'Your life is how the other person would like it to be.' If you ever find yourself dancing to someone else's tune, just stop and check your real feelings. Remember not to confuse emotional pain with being in love. If it hurts, it isn't love!

E X E R C I S E :

Changing a man

Look back at your own relationship history and think of a time when you thought you could change a man.

Complete the following statements:

1 The behaviour I wanted to change was

_____

2 I tried to change this behaviour by

_____

3 The outcome of this situation was

_____

4 My relationship with this man now is (describe the relationship)

_____

5 As a result of my attempts to change him, our relationship changed in the following ways

_____

6 Think through your answers. What conclusions can you draw?

_____

The love magnet's mantras

I am sure you have already learned from experience that you cannot change a relationship by focusing on the other person's behaviour. It's tempting to believe that things would be perfect 'if only he would change', but if we are longing for this magical moment, we may be waiting in vain for 25 years like Jerry Hall or we might waste _a whole lifetime_ in emotional pain. If you are feeling victimised in a relationship, then you have allowed this to happen. At some level you have shown the other person that this is what you think you deserve and that you are prepared to put up with it.

The great news is that you *can* change a relationship once you are prepared to change the messages you are sending to the other person. Always let your principal message be that you love and value yourself and that you deserve to be nurtured and supported and appreciated. If you expect any less than the best in love, then that is exactly what you will get. Raise your expectations: you deserve a fabulous man who is loving, supportive and sexy!

If you want to be a love magnet, choose one of the following affirmations and let it become your personal mantra for the weekend.

I, (your name) . . ., love and value myself and deserve a gorgeous man who is loving, supportive and sexy.

I, (your name) . . ., am ready for love.

Love surrounds me and supports me at all times.

My love relationships are fabulous.

It is safe for me to be myself in a love relationship.

Love makes me feel free.

Choose the mantra that most resonates with you and repeat it to yourself continually. Write it on a big piece of paper and stick it up on the wall where you can't avoid seeing it. Make a small version to keep in your pocket so that you need only to feel it to be reminded of what you truly deserve. As you work with your mantra, you will begin to change any limiting beliefs that are holding you back from attracting a great relationship. Fill your mind and soul with the amazing idea that you deserve the very best and are not prepared to settle for anything less. Yes, it's true; there is no need to sacrifice yourself to attract the love you want. If you cannot be your true self with a man, then your relationship is not built on love but on pretence. And you *can* feel free and safe when you are in love. In fact, if you don't feel like this then *it's not love*!

Stick with the same mantra for 48 hours to give it a chance to work. As you change your deep beliefs about the love that you deserve, you will radiate self-confidence and start to attract the very love you seek. A love magnet knows how to tell the difference between love and emotional pain and she has an in-built bullshit detector! In other words, she has fine powers of discrimination and

INSTANT TIP

BE A SURVIVOR

WHATEVER YOUR RELATIONSHIP HISTORY, YOU CAN ALWAYS DECIDE WHETHER TO BE A VICTIM OR A SURVIVOR. A VICTIM LOOKS BACK IN BLAME AND GIVES AWAY HER POWER TO THE PERSON WHO SHE FEELS IS RESPONSIBLE FOR HER PAIN. IF YOU BELIEVE THAT YOUR SITUATION IS SOMEONE ELSE'S FAULT THAT PERSON WILL HAVE POWER OVER YOU, BECAUSE YOU CAN ONLY WAIT FOR THEM TO CHANGE. BECOME A SURVIVOR, LET GO AND MOVE ON.

- DON'T EVER GIVE YOUR POWER AWAY. TAKE FULL RESPONSIBILITY FOR ALL YOUR ACTIONS AND DECISIONS.
- KNOW THAT YOU HAVE HELPED TO CREATE WHATEVER CIRCUMSTANCES YOU FIND YOURSELF IN.
- RECOGNISE THAT WHATEVER HAPPENED IN YOUR RELATIONSHIP IS NOT A REFLECTION OF YOUR WORTH AS A PERSON.
- FIND A WAY TO LET GO AND MOVE ON. LOVE YOURSELF FOR YOUR GRIT AND DETERMINATION TO SURVIVE AND CONQUER!
- REMIND YOURSELF THAT EVERYTHING HAPPENS FOR A REASON AND THAT A RELATIONSHIP BREAK-UP IS

> NOT THE END OF THE WORLD (ALTHOUGH IT MIGHT
> FEEL LIKE IT FOR A WHILE).
> - STOP ANY NEGATIVE OR SELF-CRITICAL THOUGHTS
>   AND JUST REMEMBER WHAT A GREAT GIRL YOU ARE.
> - YOU DESERVE A WONDERFUL RELATIONSHIP; YOU
>   ARE WORTH IT. KEEP TELLING YOURSELF THIS.
> - DON'T ACT LIKE A VICTIM AND YOU WON'T FEEL
>   LIKE ONE.

can sniff out a man who would not be right for her. So often we end up in emotional entanglements only to say something like, 'Why did I ever get into this?' or 'I should have seen this coming.'

A love magnet doesn't let her feelings override her reason and neither does she deny her instincts; she uses her head and her heart to make decisions. Work with your mantra and just watch your love dilemmas resolve as you begin to trust your own judgement and act upon it.

What sort of men are you attracting?

A few months ago I spent a Saturday night with a friend who has just begun a relationship with a new man. She is an intelligent woman with a high-flying career and a heart of gold, but she is also utterly desperate to have a long-term relationship. All night I listened to how great this guy was and what he thought about every subject under the sun. No topic was safe; somehow she made sure that every conversation led back to him. I knew that he was often moody and critical, but she excused all his bad behaviour, revealing to me the fascinating details of his 'unhappy childhood' and his 'dominating mother'. My clever and interesting friend had attracted a self-opinionated bore of a man and she was fast turning into a bore herself.

It's so easy to look at other people's relationships and see what's going on, isn't it? Why did it take so long for Jerry to realise that Mick was never going to change his philandering ways? We know for sure that we wouldn't stay with a man like that, however talented, dynamic and funny he was. But it's much harder to get clear about our own love lives; we have made such a large emotional investment and sometimes we just can't see the wood for the trees (or the great guys for the love rats).

EXERCISE:
Your love choices

If you have not started to use a notebook for your thoughts and reflections, then wait no longer. This is a key exercise for you, and one we shall refer to later, so get out your love journal.

1 List the names of all the men who you have had a significant relationship with in the past, including your present relationship if you have one. Leave plenty of space after each name.

2 Then, after each name make a list of that man's negative qualities – the things you most disliked about him. Just use one or two words for your description. For example, Alana's boyfriend always criticised her dress sense, her ideas and, well, just about everything about her – she wrote the word 'critical' to describe this behaviour. Do not include any positive qualities here.

3 Look back at your lists and highlight any qualities or words that appear in more than one list.

4 Write a list of all the repeating words and qualities.

5 Look at this final list and spend a few moments reflecting on the nature of your significant relationships.

6 Now ask yourself the following questions:

- Are there any patterns in my relationships?
- Have I attracted some negative qualities more than once?
- Do I make a habit of going for men with certain types of behaviour?
- Are my relationships getting healthier or worse or are they all much the same?
- What are the key negative qualities I seem to attract?
- What does this exercise tell me about myself and the sort of men I have drawn into my life?

I haven't forgotten that these men also have plenty of positive qualities (why else would you have been with them?). But for the moment we are just looking for reasons why your love choices might not have worked. Many clients are very embarrassed by this exercise, finding it hard to believe that men who seemed so different from each other at the outset, in the end displayed such similar negative patterns. But knowledge is power, and the more you can find out about what doesn't work for you, the clearer you become about what does. For example, if one of your key repeating negative qualities is 'emotionally withdrawn', you know from now on that this type is not good for you. Alana, 36 and a primary school teacher, was at first horrified by the results of this exercise; she found the word 'critical' in every one of her six lists (the last one being her present relationship). On reflection Alana recognised that her own self-criticism had kept these relationships in place; she had *believed* that she deserved to be criticised and so she attracted men who put her down. Alana started to use the love magnet's mantras and began to work on her self-belief and self-confidence. As she found new inner strength, she refused to put up with the constant disapproval of her partner, telling him that if he couldn't treat her with the respect that she deserved then it was finished between them. Over the course of the next six months Alana taught him how to treat her well, and their relationship has gone from strength to strength. So don't despair when you recognise repeating negative patterns in your relationships; this is valuable information which you can use to transform and heal your love life.

Love magnets are always ready for love

You will only have great relationships when you are ready to take responsibility for yourself. Once you accept that the qualities of your thoughts and beliefs help to create the quality of your life, you are well on your way to going for and achieving whatever it is you want. A positive approach keeps you motivated and enthusiastic, and this energy always attracts fresh possibilities and new relationships. Yes, there really are many more fish in the sea; you just have to get out there with your rod! The negative view will create self-doubt and insecurity and an inability to take assertive action, so if a likely love interest

INSTANT TIP

LEARNING FROM THE PAST

- BE POSITIVE ABOUT ALL YOUR PAST RELATIONSHIPS.
- INSTEAD OF VIEWING THEM AS FAILURES, SEEK TO DISCOVER EXACTLY WHAT WENT WRONG AND WHY. IT TAKES TWO TO MAKE OR BREAK A RELATIONSHIP, SO UNDERSTAND THE PARTS YOU BOTH PLAYED.
- FORGIVE YOURSELF AND YOUR EX-PARTNERS AND YOU WILL FEEL FREE TO MOVE ON AND CREATE A NEW AND VIBRANT RELATIONSHIP.
- ONCE YOU HAVE A CLEAR VISION OF WHAT YOU NOW WANT AND EXPECT FROM LOVE, YOU CAN CREATE SOME NEW, EXCITING AND POSITIVE RELATIONSHIP GOALS.
- RADIATE 100 PER CENT SELF-BELIEF AND YOU WILL ACHIEVE THESE GOALS.

does swim by, it might be just too scary to bait your line and reel him in.

Whether your thoughts and beliefs are positive or negative will obviously have a great impact on the type of people you attract and the sort of relationship choices you make. Your attitude determines your mood. An optimistic outlook always brings a feeling of hopefulness and confidence to any situation, and this automatically opens the door to new prospects in life (and love). You always have the freedom to choose your attitude, although this may be hard to remember when you are feeling low. It's simple: negativity attracts negativity, and positivity attracts positivity. So radiate whatever it is you want to attract. When you demonstrate enthusiasm and motivation, you uplift the energy of those around you and draw similarly positive people into your orbit. The type of relationships you attract depends entirely upon the type of energy you project.

As in life coaching so in love coaching: we get clear about what we want by specifying our goals and then creating an easy step-by-step action plan. Take an assertive approach to your love life and start thinking about your relationship goals. We will look at this in more detail later, but for now just begin to visualise what you really want. Perhaps you enjoy the single life and would love an uncomplicated sexy liaison, or maybe you just need to revitalise your present relationship. If you feel ready for a long-term commitment, obviously your situation is different from that of someone who is playing the field and just enjoying the dating game. Clients are often amazed when I ask them about their relationship goals, as if love is something that 'just happens to happen'. But I say this: how can you catch the fish you want if you are in the wrong waters, or you haven't got a fishing rod, or you have the wrong bait? Forward planning, good technique and clever strategy makes it possible to achieve our life goals. Apply exactly the same methodology to your love goals, then when love 'just happens' (as it will) you will be absolutely ready to go for it. Love magnets are always ready for love!

MEDITATION MOMENT

VISUALISING YOUR POWERFUL ENERGY

GET COMFORTABLE, CLOSE YOUR EYES AND RELAX. CONCENTRATE ON YOUR BREATHING. GRADUALLY YOU WILL FEEL CALMER AS YOUR BREATHS BECOME SLOWER AND STEADIER AND YOUR STRESS AND STRAINS DROP AWAY.

WHEN YOU ARE READY, BRING AN IMAGE OF YOURSELF INTO YOUR MIND'S EYE. IMAGINE THAT YOU ARE FILLED WITH POWERFUL, POSITIVE, MAGNETIC ENERGY. NOTICE THAT THE ENERGY SURROUNDING YOUR BODY (YOUR AURA) IS GLOWING RADIANTLY. YOU ARE RESONATING FORCEFUL AND CHARISMATIC ENERGY THAT YOU HAVE CREATED BY DEVELOPING YOUR INNER STRENGTH. EACH POSITIVE BELIEVE, EACH

SELF-AFFIRMING THOUGHT AND EVERY POSITIVE ACTION CREATES STRONG ENERGY THAT RADIATES IN YOUR AURA. SEE THE PERSONAL POWER THAT YOU GENERATE.

NOW FEEL THE ENERGY AROUND YOUR BODY. IN YOUR MIND TRACE THE OUTLINE OF YOUR AURA, WHICH YOU WILL FEEL A FEW CENTIMETRES BEYOND YOUR BODY. DON'T WORRY IF YOU CAN'T FEEL ANYTHING; JUST KNOW THAT IT IS THERE. FOLLOW YOUR AURA FROM THE TOP OF YOUR HEAD DOWN TO YOUR SHOULDER, THEN AROUND THE OUTLINE OF YOUR ARM AND THEN DOWN TO YOUR HIP AND AROUND YOUR LEG AND SO ON UNTIL YOU RETURN TO YOUR STARTING POINT.

WHEN YOU HAVE COMPLETED THE CIRCUIT, TUNE IN TO YOUR AURA AND FEEL THE POSITIVE VIBRATIONS THAT YOU ARE CARRYING. YOU MAY FEEL A TINGLING SENSATION OR YOU MAY FEEL AN ENERGY SURGE OR YOU MAY FEEL NOTHING AT ALL. WHATEVER HAPPENS, JUST *KNOW* THAT YOUR POWERFUL AURA IS RADIATING STRONG POSITIVE SIGNALS. SIT WITH THIS FEELING FOR A MOMENT.

WHEN YOU OPEN YOUR EYES, JUST REMEMBER THAT YOU ARE *STILL* RADIATING THIS ENERGY. REMAIN CONSCIOUS OF IT THROUGHOUT YOUR DAY. TUNE IN TO YOUR OWN MAGNETIC BROADCAST SIMPLY BY INCREASING YOUR AWARENESS OF IT. AS YOU DO THIS, YOUR ENERGY WILL INCREASE AND YOU WILL ATTRACT THE MOST WONDERFUL POSITIVE SITUATIONS AND PEOPLE INTO YOUR ORBIT.

BECOME AWARE OF THE POWERFUL ENERGY THAT YOU
TRANSMIT AND YOU WILL DRAW POSITIVE VIBRATIONS
INTO YOUR LIFE. LOVE MAGNETS CONSCIOUSLY BROAD-
CAST THEIR OWN POSITIVE MAGNETISM.

Step 3
Find Romance

And if you look for it, I've got a sneaking suspicion that love actually is all around.

HUGH GRANT AS THE PRIME MINISTER
IN THE FILM *LOVE ACTUALLY*

Richard Curtis is the brilliantly talented writer and producer who gave us the films *Four Weddings and a Funeral*, *Notting Hill* and *Love Actually*. All the women I know (and secretly most of the men) are happy to watch these movies over and over again. Of course they are great entertainment with their glossy formats and star-studded casts, but the main attraction is their subject matter. These films are all about the search for romance; the eternal quest for that elusive, magical state that we call love. And we all so love to love! Everyone is a romantic at heart.

When you lose your appetite, feel too excited to sleep and just can't wait for the moment when you will hear his voice again, you are in the first throes of romance! What an amazing feeling it is; it elevates and inspires us and changes the way we think, feel and behave. Our daily life can become an almost mystical experience when we look upon our sweetheart, and the rest of the world, through the eyes of passion. It's hardly surprising that some of us have become addicted to falling in love.

Truly, madly and deeply in love

A recent neuroscientific research project studied a group of men and women who described themselves as being 'truly, madly and deeply' in love. The participants were asked to look at a picture of their beloved while undergoing a brainscan. The results showed activity in the four areas of the brain that also become activated during drug-induced euphoria. In other words love is a drug! Dr John Marsden of the Institute of Psychiatry in London says that the 'lust' stage of a relationship 'produces the same responses in the brain as taking cocaine'.

When you fall in love, your brain is flooded with a potent cocktail of hormones which increase your levels of alertness and sharpen your senses. At the same time you experience a rush of phenylethylamine (PEA), which is a mood elevator that raises your energy and causes you to be less aware of your partner's faults. PEA peaks for about 6 months and is responsible for your enhanced sexual appetite. All this sex increases the levels of the hormones DHEA and oestrogen, which in turn increase your metabolic rate and encourage weight loss. High levels of oestrogen also give a wonderful bloom to your skin and make your hair thicker and glossier. So you not only feel good but you look fantastic too! PEA levels eventually fall away, so enjoy the chemical buzz while it lasts, but accept that you will not be able to depend on the 'lover's high' to keep your relationship sizzling forever. When the lust phase ends, you will need to have developed other areas of your relationship if you are to keep your romance alive.

Jo, 35, is an internet entrepreneur who describes herself as 'a woman with sophisticated tastes in men'. She has had many flings with educated and interesting partners, but in the past none of them has lasted longer than six months. Jo met Adam (a furniture designer) when she was working in New York. They hit it off straight away and she came back to London full of the excitement of her new affair.

When Adam came to visit her, Jo realised that he was taking their relationship seriously and that he was very committed to her. This took away the light-hearted buzz she loves so much, and would normally have led her to end the affair. Jo came for coaching because she felt that maybe this relationship would go further if she could only give it a chance, but she felt too afraid to try. Her pattern was to fall in love and enjoy the exhilaration and great sex that comes in the 'getting to know' phase and then, as soon as this started to wear off, move on and look for someone else. She talked about her 'addiction' to love and how this was stopping her developing a long-term relationship with anyone. Jo said, 'I have always been afraid to get to know someone at a deeper level, but now that I have met Adam I am more afraid of losing him.'

After we had looked at her past patterns, Jo focused on creating some relationship goals. One of her goals was to develop the level of intimacy between the two of them, and she decided that the first step would be to talk to Adam about her fears. This was the first time that Jo had ever disclosed so much emotional information to a man, and her trust in him paid off. He said that he also felt scared of making a deeper commitment but that he knew that he wanted to be with her more than anything and was prepared to give it a go. This conversation took them both on to a new level of intimacy with each other, and they have been together now for about three years. Jo said that she had to break her addiction in order to discover how wonderful a deep and trusting relationship can be.

Love addiction: are you at risk?

Are you in love with being in love? I think it's fair to say that we all want love in our lives. Most of us would like a powerful, sexy and enduring romance with a wonderful man. But sometimes our desire to be in love can turn us into 'love junkies'. The important thing to remember is that lust is blind. In those first heady days, as your PEA levels shoot through the ceiling, your love choices, decisions and judgements are suspect: you are not your usual self and may not be for a few months.

As time passes and the love drug becomes less effective, you may find yourself hooked in a slightly different way. You may have embarked on the next stage of the relationship only to discover that you have been obsessing about a totally unsuitable man. Sounds crazy? Well, actually it's very common. We have all been there at one time or another. Most of us have made relationship mistakes, and women do so love to try to change a challenging man. It can be hard for us to accept that our love object is not who we thought he was or who we want him to be, and sometimes we will spend years trying to alter him. This is another form of love addiction.

Try the love addiction exercise below to check whether you are at risk of addiction to love.

EXERCISE:

Love addiction risk assessment

Read the following statements and tick those that apply to you.

- You have been head over heels and high on love.
- You have moved on to a new affair as soon as the fireworks stopped, and you have repeated this pattern a number of times.
- You have chased after a man when he withdrew his attention (continually contacting him and trying to make things right).
- You have compromised yourself sexually to please a partner.
- You have stopped going out with friends and stayed in waiting for a lover to call.
- You have turned a blind eye to a partner's shortcomings and excused his bad behaviour.
- You have stayed in a relationship after your partner abused you physically, mentally or emotionally.

- You have felt that only your lover could fill the empty space inside you.
- You have continually wondered about what your lover thought of you.
- You have stayed with a man who was critical.
- You have felt low in self-confidence while in a relationship.
- You have been in a relationship in which you were always trying to please your partner.
- You have been together with a man who was emotionally withdrawn.

Have you shown any of the symptoms of love addiction?

Perhaps you are feeling addicted to love right now. If so, don't despair; it is not a fatal condition! In fact, as soon as you get wise to the way you get hooked on certain men, you learn something very important about yourself and your behaviour in relationships. This information leads to increased self-awareness, enabling you to change your negative patterns, grow in self-confidence and begin to magnetise the love you deserve.

INSTANT TIP

APPRAISE YOUR RELATIONSHIP PROSPECTS

INTIMATE LOVE RELATIONSHIPS CAN ONLY WORK WHEN BOTH PARTNERS HAVE A STRONG SENSE OF SELF-WORTH.

If you enter a relationship in a vulnerable state (on the rebound/feeling needy), you will lack the confidence to be yourself, and this will eventually lead to problems. Before you embark on a new relationship ask yourself the following questions:

- Am I feeling needy?

- Is this a good relationship choice?

- Does he respect me?

- Am I at ease with him or am I on edge?

- Do I feel safe with him?

- Is he trustworthy and reliable?

- Do I respect him?

- Is he needy?

- What are his positive qualities?

- What are his negative qualities?

- Am I happy with myself?

- Is he happy with himself?

- Do I need to resolve any personal issues before I commit to a new relationship?

Consider your answers. What do they reveal about the possibilities for this relationship? Be guided by your clear, cool appraisal.

Romantic love

Of course we want to have amazing sex, to go weak at the knees when we see him, to be courted and openly appreciated, and to feel that we are his number one priority. We want champagne, chocolates and flowers, but we also need a lot more if this is to be the romantic love relationship of our dreams. Courtney Cox, speaking of her great relationship with her husband, David Arquette, says, 'With David I just lucked out that I found someone who's sexy and who's also there for me.' And this, in a nutshell, is exactly what we all want. If he's 'there for you' but you are not sexually drawn to him, then he can only be a good friend; and if the sex is great but he's not there for you, then this is lust not love. Don't confuse romance with an unattainable fantasy that you will only see on the screen or read about in novels.

If you want romance, you have to draw it into your life with your powerful, upbeat personal magnetism. Remember how a love magnet never allows herself to be a victim of love? This means that she knows what she wants from a relationship and doesn't settle for anything less; she aims high and expects the best. And this is exactly what you must do if you want real love in your life; you must attract romance at the mental, physical and emotional levels. Be warned: if one of the components is missing, then at some level this relationship will hurt you, and if it hurts it can't be love! When you are with him you are a meeting of minds, bodies and emotions. Check out how well he scores in the total attraction stakes.

How attractive is he?

Answer the following questions and see how mentally, physically and emotionally attractive you find your man. Score as follows:

(a) = 0
(b) = 2
(c) = 6
(d) = 8

MENTALLY

1   If he is feeling a bit low does he:
(a)   Get moody and cross and complain.
(b)   Refuse to discuss it with you.
(c)   Try to take a positive approach and not let it get him down.
(d)   Talk to you about it and feel more upbeat afterwards.

2   You would describe him as a man who:
(a)   Is often very negative.
(b)   Is sometimes low in confidence and self-belief.
(c)   Tries to keep as upbeat as possible.
(d)   Is always able to keep things in perspective and knows how to value himself.

PHYSICALLY

1 Is your sex life:

(a) Often disappointing.

(b) Average, nothing to write home about.

(c) Exciting and sizzling.

(d) Exciting and sizzling and also comforting and reassuring.

2 Would you describe him physically as:

(a) OK.

(b) Quite attractive.

(c) Your type of man.

(d) A gorgeous sexy hunk.

EMOTIONALLY

1 Would you describe him as a man who:

(a) Is emotionally withdrawn.

(b) Isn't in touch with his feelings but recognises your feelings.

(c) Tries to express his emotions but finds it very hard.

(d) Knows how he feels most of the time and is prepared to bare his soul to you.

2 When you express your feelings does he:

(a) Shut down or get angry.

(b) Listen but not know how to respond.

(c) Let you have your say and try to come up with solutions.

(d) Just listen to you and give you the emotional support that you need.

If you scored 0–12
He is struggling in the total attraction stakes, and you know it. This relationship is a difficult one, and romance is not part of it.

If you scored 14–26
Romance is not blooming yet, although there is a glimmer of hope. He has his moments, but you wish there were more of them.

If you scored 28–38
This might be love. His energy attracts you at some levels, and you can build on this. Show him how much you appreciate the effort he puts into your relationship and this will encourage him further. When he trusts you, mentally, physically and emotionally he will become your Romeo.

If you scored 40–48
He has what it takes to keep you satisfied at all levels; he is sexy and he is there for you. Lucky girl! Hang on to him. He is romantic love material, but I'm sure you don't need me to tell you this.

Your personal love plan

Actress Julianne Moore says: 'You have to make a positive effort to nurture romance – it's not something that just happens to you.' You can find romance and have a successful relationship but only if you set about it the right way. While love (lust) at first sight might be a good start (it shows that the sexual chemistry is there between you), you will be aware that it takes more than this to

INSTANT TIP

ROMANCE CHECKLIST

ROMANCE IS . . .

- TAKING CARE OF EACH OTHER
- FEELING THAT YOU ARE BEST FRIENDS
- KNOWING THAT HE IS ALWAYS ON YOUR SIDE
- BEING ABLE TO BE YOURSELF
- SAYING WHAT YOU FEEL AND KNOWING HE WILL LISTEN
- KEEPING YOUR SEX LIFE FRESH AND INVIGORATING
- ADMITTING WHEN YOU ARE WRONG
- LETTING HIM OFF THE HOOK
- CONFIDING IN EACH OTHER
- BEING HIS NUMBER ONE PRIORITY
- KEEPING INTERESTED IN EACH OTHER'S LIVES
- SHOWING THAT YOU LOVE EACH OTHER EVERY DAY
- VALUING YOUR RELATIONSHIP AND WORKING ON IT
- STICKING IN THERE EVEN WHEN IT GETS TOUGH
- REMEMBERING TO KEEP THE FLAME ALIVE
- FEELING CHERISHED

develop a lasting and intimate relationship. Successful outcomes always depend upon focus, clarity, motivation and a realistic action plan. Again, love coaching borrows from the techniques of life coaching. Use this simple six-point plan to help you to clarify your love goals and to set about achieving them.

1 State your goals

What are your love goals? We are usually so wound up with our relationship 'problems' that it comes as some surprise to think of taking an assertive role and focusing on what we want rather than what we are getting. As soon as you specify your goals and write them down, you have taken the first vital step towards achieving them. Spend some time thinking this through. What do you want? Would you like to get out and meet more new men? Do you want to have more fun in your relationship? Perhaps you would like to enhance the way you communicate with each other. Do you want to improve the level of trust between you? Would you like to be able to express your needs more clearly? Are you looking for a long-term commitment? Write your goals in your journal and make sure they are positive. Begin each one with *I want* . . . You may be surprised to discover what exactly it is you do want!

2 Keep positively focused

Focus on your targets and take a step towards them every day. This creates self-confidence and gives you love magnet status. So, for example, if you are looking for a new relationship, you could change your usual social habits and visit different places and locations. Get out and about and remember that you are unlikely to meet your dream man in a bar. Do something every day towards increasing your chances of meeting someone new. When you work towards achieving any desired aim, your dynamic energy attracts positive outcomes. This works for love just as it does for the rest of life.

Repeat the love magnet's mantras on page 37 to keep your energy high. Don't worry if you find it hard to believe these powerful positive love affirmations; they work at the very deepest level of your being and replace those negative beliefs that have stopped you attracting the love you want. Bring your positive thoughts about love and relationships right into the centre of your life and you will see them come true. You *do* deserve a fantastic love life. Keep reminding yourself of this.

3 See yourself as a love magnet

When you change your negative self-image by filling your mind with positive thoughts about yourself, you attract new vibrant energy into your life (and your love life). But just as positive thoughts help you to reach new love goals, so do the mental images that you carry in your head. Whatever you continually 'see' in your mind's eye will eventually come true for you in some way. So let go of any negative images that stop you from becoming a love magnet. See yourself as being lucky in love; don't ever imagine that you are a victim. You are a survivor, so see yourself bouncing back again and again if necessary.

Cultivate an image of yourself as a person who knows her own mind and dances to her own tune. You are an independent woman with unique talents and strengths. Be sure that the pictures of yourself you carry in your head fit with this description. When you say the love magnet's mantras, picture yourself radiating and attracting positive love vibrations. Stand in front of the mirror and practise exuding self-confidence and charisma; create these new pictures of yourself as a love goddess and before very long you will become one!

4 Visualise your goals

Surrounding yourself with positive self-images reminds you of who you really are and what you deserve. But visualisation takes you further than this, into an entirely new level of awareness; it actually helps to *imprint* your new goals firmly in your mind.

Find a quiet place where you will be undisturbed for a few minutes. Relax and close your eyes. Imagine that you are looking at an empty white screen and that you are now going to create your very own action movie. Visualise yourself going for your love goals and being successful; see yourself looking good and feeling fabulous. Make the pictures vivid and bright and add a great soundtrack. Hear the admiration in the voices of others, see the appreciation in the eyes of the people around you, notice how you effortlessly draw their attention. Imagine being in a loving relationship and see yourself really living this reality. Be creative with this film and let your attractive energy really flow. Let your film be supportive, positive and realistic. Now whenever you have a quiet moment you can re-create these screen images in a flash; they are imprinted on your mind. Keep practising this technique, because it reinforces all the other steps you are taking.

5 Be your own best friend

You create the reality that you expect; people and events walk through the doors of your expectations. This means that you are the director of your own life. You are the only person who can make your dreams come true. If you are self-critical and negative, you will attract relationships that reflect these harmful beliefs. Treat yourself the way you treat your best friend. Whenever she is down, you are encouraging, and when she is up, you celebrate her victories with her. Now do the same for yourself. Notice how you speak to yourself and keep the commentary positive and motivating. Uplift your energy and tell yourself how well you are doing. When you remind yourself that 'You can do it', you are affirming your resolution and willpower, and nothing can beat that! You are a winner in life and love, and don't let yourself forget it.

6 Go for it!

Now bring together all your techniques to create a quick and easy routine that you can repeat throughout the day. Choose the love mantras and matching self-images that feel appropriate for you. Run your visualisation movie across the screen in your head and really get into the feelings it evokes. Keep your inner talk confident and loving and let yourself off any restraining hooks that you might be hanging from (this just means forgiving yourself).

In other words, just think, feel and see love all around you, because of course it is always there; you only need to know how to draw it into your orbit.

The greatest romance of your life

In her heart-warming book for women *Romancing the Ordinary*, Sarah Ban Breathnach writes: 'Believe me, you will never find a lover who will adore, desire, caress, embrace and delight you more than Life. So give me a few minutes a day to chat Life up on your behalf.' Sarah encourages us to delight in the often overlooked pleasures of every day. She shows us how to seduce the most important person in our lives – ourselves. Her lovely book is full of tempting treats and seasonal indulgences, as well as pampering beauty treatments and sexy secret pleasures.

So don't stash away your new Agent Provocateur underwear for when the right moment occurs; get it out now and wear it to work. Put on your killer heels and strut your stuff. Act glamorous and you will be glamorous! You could take yourself on a date, join a belly dancing class, read a novel in the bath, create an exotic meal for one . . . the possibilities are endless. What is it that you would really *love* to do? Give yourself permission to get out there and bring it into your life. The more you can love your life the more it will love you back so start to love it *now*! And, of course, as soon as you can fully appreciate yourself, your energy will become charismatic. Romance your everyday moments and treat yourself like a goddess and let love enter your life. Remember that love actually *is* all around.

MEDITATION MOMENT

LOVING YOUR LIFE

RELAX, CLOSE YOUR EYES AND STEADY YOUR BREATHING. LET GO OF ALL YOUR PHYSICAL TENSION. LET GO OF ALL YOUR MENTAL TENSION AND FEEL YOURSELF DROPPING INTO A CALM PLACE DEEP INSIDE YOU.

AS YOU SIT, QUIETLY BRING TO MIND ALL THE SIMPLE THINGS IN YOUR LIFE THAT YOU LOVE AND APPRECIATE. SOME EXAMPLES FROM CLIENTS ARE:

- THE SMELL OF ROSES
- FRESHLY LAUNDERED SHEETS
- MY MOTHER'S SMILE
- SNOW IN THE MOONLIGHT
- PAPERS IN BED ON A SUNDAY MORNING
- CHRISTMAS CAROLS
- AUNT ELLEN'S CHOCOLATE CAKE
- TAKING A SAUNA
- MAKING SANDCASTLES ON THE BEACH

- THE HAIRS ON THE BACK OF MY BABY'S NECK
- MY BEST FRIEND'S LAUGH
- THE SMELL OF FRESHLY GROUND COFFEE
- SITTING IN THE SUNSHINE
- TAKING MY DOG FOR A WALK

NOW OPEN YOUR EYES AND WRITE YOUR OWN LIST IN YOUR LOVE JOURNAL. THE WONDERFUL THING ABOUT AN APPRECIATION LIST IS THAT AS SOON AS YOU START WRITING, MORE AND MORE THINGS COME INTO YOUR HEAD. IT'S ALMOST AS IF YOUR FEELINGS OF APPRECIATION AND LOVE OPEN A DOOR FOR ALL THE GOOD THINGS IN LIFE TO ENTER.

REFLECT ON YOUR LIST AND GIVE THANKS FOR ALL THE GIFTS THAT YOU RECEIVE EVERY DAY. GET INTO THE LOVE AND APPRECIATION HABIT AND ALL ASPECTS OF YOUR LIFE WILL BECOME MORE AND MORE WONDERFUL. REMEMBER THAT YOU ATTRACT WHATEVER YOU RADIATE. DEMONSTRATE LOVE AND APPRECIATION, AND YOU WILL ATTRACT LOVE AND APPRECIATION!

Step 4
Take Charge of Your Love Life

Sometimes it's hard to be assertive when we're wired to want love and to please.

NIKKI GEMMELL

As US Secretary of State, Madeleine Albright was once one of the world's most influential women. She was in charge of the foreign policy of the most powerful nation on earth, and thus we might easily conclude that she is a woman who certainly knows her own mind. But recently, talking about being a wife, she had this to say: 'In the 23 years I was married to Joe, his tastes became mine. After he left, I rediscovered the fact that I didn't like beef – even though for years we had eaten it almost every night.'

We needn't be so surprised by this confession; haven't we all compromised ourselves at some time to keep our intimate relationship running smoothly? How many times have you capitulated to your partner for the greater good of peace and harmony on the love front? I have had many clients who have described themselves as being 'assertive' in every area of their lives except in their intimate relationships. Most of these women were in high-profile jobs in which they needed strong self-belief and high levels of self-esteem to operate efficiently every day; they were in control in the workplace, but their love lives were in a mess. As Ms Albright demonstrates so beautifully, it is only too easy for us to lose sight of our assertiveness as we cross over the threshold into our role as lover and partner.

Sex columnist Nikki Gemmell is right; we are indeed 'wired to want love and to please'. But, girls, although we may well be programmed to act like this, it certainly doesn't mean that there is no other alternative open to us. Of course, relationships are all about give and take, but we just have to make sure that we are not the ones who are doing all the giving!

Have you got relationship self-esteem?

Taking control of our love lives requires that we take a close look at the ways we behave in our intimate relationships. It is not smart to leave our assertive self behind at work and to allow ourselves to be severely compromised at home. There is a direct link between your behaviour and your levels of relationship self-esteem.

If you are low in relationship self-esteem, you are a victim of love, and you will be:

- Unable to make good relationship decisions
- Addicted to the idea of love
- Waiting for a love interest to change
- Believing that you deserve the treatment you are getting
- Living with low expectations of yourself and of your partner
- Giving and not taking
- Unhappy with yourself

If you are high in relationship self-esteem, you are a love magnet, and you will be:

- Making good relationship decisions
- Setting positive love goals
- Dancing to your own tune
- Believing that you deserve a fabulous, nurturing relationship
- Living with high expectations of yourself and of your partner
- Giving and taking in equal measure
- Happy with yourself

You attract exactly the type of love relationship that you are ready for. Who and what are you ready to attract right now? Look at the diagram on page 73 to check exactly how you behave in your interactions with your loved one. Are you acting like a love magnet or are you behaving like a love victim?

A love magnet always behaves assertively

More important than *what* you do is *how* you do it. The diagram on page 73 shows the range of behaviour that is open to us in any of our interactions in our love relationships. If you want a great outcome, you need to understand the way that different behavioural styles work.

When you and your lover are communicating, you are engaged in a **love interaction** (see the centre of the diagram). A **love magnet** behaves **assertively** and knows what she wants and what she doesn't want from her relationship, and she is ready to make this clear. Are you behaving assertively in your love interactions? Have you got the confidence to go for your relationship goals? How are your communication skills? Do you know how to express your real feelings? Check the list of assertive behavioural qualities shown in the diagram.

A **love victim** behaves **aggressively** or **submissively** or anywhere in between. She gets angry and resentful and will often blame her lover for their relationship difficulties. She is afraid to show her feelings and finds it hard to communicate effectively. She is insecure and low on self-respect. The diagram shows a two-way arrow between aggressive and submissive behaviour. This is because the love victim often swings between these two extremes.

Paula, 42, is an artist who has fiery roller-coaster love affairs that always fizzle out very quickly. Her first love is her painting, and she freely admits that she really can't be bothered to put any time into developing a good relationship. She is a brilliant example of a woman who lurches

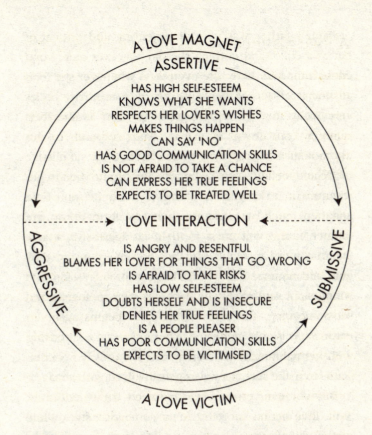

A LOVE MAGNET

ASSERTIVE

HAS HIGH SELF-ESTEEM
KNOWS WHAT SHE WANTS
RESPECTS HER LOVER'S WISHES
MAKES THINGS HAPPEN
CAN SAY 'NO'
HAS GOOD COMMUNICATION SKILLS
IS NOT AFRAID TO TAKE A CHANCE
CAN EXPRESS HER TRUE FEELINGS
EXPECTS TO BE TREATED WELL

LOVE INTERACTION

AGGRESSIVE

SUBMISSIVE

IS ANGRY AND RESENTFUL
BLAMES HER LOVER FOR THINGS THAT GO WRONG
IS AFRAID TO TAKE RISKS
HAS LOW SELF-ESTEEM
DOUBTS HERSELF AND IS INSECURE
DENIES HER TRUE FEELINGS
IS A PEOPLE PLEASER
HAS POOR COMMUNICATION SKILLS
EXPECTS TO BE VICTIMISED

A LOVE VICTIM

from submission to aggression and back again. Paula's last affair was with Jack, 54, who runs his own management consultancy and was fascinated and enchanted by Paula's tempestuous creative spirit. But after three months of living with her uncertain and unpredictable moods he left, saying that she was 'too much like hard work' and that he never knew where he was with her. Paula is always secretly relieved when her romances end, because she feels that she can then get back to some serious work.

Paula's father was very domineering and critical of her as a child, and nothing she did was ever quite good enough for him. Now she overreacts whenever she feels anyone is criticising her, and this over-sensitivity bodes very badly for her relationships. As soon as she feels remotely 'put down' by a man, Paula responds to this psychological 'threat' by withdrawing into the submissive mode and feeling sorry for herself. She can hold on to her resentment in her quiet brooding way for quite some time and then, much later (and usually at a totally inappropriate moment), she will burst forth in an aggressive attack. Eventually and inevitably, she then becomes consumed by guilt and remorse and swings back from aggression into submission. And so, as she becomes over-apologetic and self-demeaning, the love victim cycle begins again. In truth, Paula is only interested in her long-term relationship with her painting, and I suspect that she uses her 'victim' status to make sure she never gets involved with a man.

But not everyone swings between these extremes. Some love victims specialise in the submissive style, while others use aggressive tactics. At first it might seem that these two styles are completely different. An aggressor is loud and domineering and may appear to be determined and confident, in contrast to the submissive person, who has a quiet approach and seems to lack confidence and direction. However, both styles are manipulative and blaming, and they are both ineffective.

Do you recognise these behaviour patterns? Do you know someone who is submissive? Have you ever had a love relationship with someone like this? Do you know anyone who is aggressive in their intimate relationships? Perhaps you know a couple in which one plays the submissive role while the other plays the aggressor. These behavioural styles often attract each other, and they dance a merry (victim) dance together. And who do you know who is assertive? What sort of love relationships does this person have?

We have all behaved in these three modes at one time or another in our love lives. If we are feeling low in self-confidence, we will find ourselves somewhere in the victim category, whether submissive or aggressive; when our self-esteem is low we can only act as love victims. When we are feeling good about ourselves, we can act assertively and use positive communication skills to create a close and intimate relationship with our partner. When our self-esteem is high, we can only operate in a non-victim mode, and we become love magnets.

EXERCISE:

Reviewing your relationship behaviour

Can you think of a time when you have behaved in each of these three ways in a love relationship?

1 A time when I behaved submissively

The situation was:

_____

The way I behaved was:

_____

The outcome of the situation was:

_____

2 A time when I behaved aggressively

The situation was:

_____

The way I behaved was:

_____

The outcome of the situation was:

_____

3 A time when I behaved assertively

The situation was:

_____

The way I behaved was:

_____

The outcome of the situation was:

_____

What do your answers show you about how your behaviour affected your love interactions? Can you see how your victim-like behaviour in situations one and two created a poor outcome? What do you think would have happened if you had acted assertively? Look again at situation three and consider what your assertive behaviour actually was. For example you might have:

- Said what you meant
- Stood up for yourself
- Negotiated your outcome
- Listened to your partner
- Tried to understand his point of view
- Communicated your needs clearly and without being critical
- Demonstrated your belief that you could work things out together

My two marriages

When my first marriage ended I was full of anger with my ex-husband. I could clearly see that he had treated me badly. He eventually played away, and I was firmly fixed in my role as wronged wife and dutiful mother. As time has passed, I have looked back at our relationship with the benefit of hindsight and also of the set of assertiveness skills that I have since learned. The truth is that I was 50 per cent to blame for the failure of our relationship.

I had lived with Ian for three years before we got married, and we were good friends who loved each other.

Things began to go wrong when he set up a new antiques business at the same time as our first child was born. Twenty months later I gave birth again, but by then our paths were already separating: he was absorbed with the

---

INSTANT TIP

BE YOURSELF

WHEN YOU FEEL FREE TO BE YOURSELF, YOU ARE CONFIDENT AND ASSERTIVE IN ALL OF YOUR RELATIONSHIPS. BEING YOURSELF ALWAYS MEANS BEING IN TOUCH WITH YOUR THOUGHTS, FEELINGS AND BEHAVIOUR, SO START TO BECOME AWARE OF THESE THROUGHOUT THE DAY.

- YOUR THOUGHTS – EVERY NOW AND AGAIN STOP AND REFLECT FOR A MOMENT. ASK YOURSELF, 'WHAT DO I REALLY THINK?' THE MORE YOU DO THIS, THE MORE YOU WILL GET TO KNOW YOUR OWN MIND.
- YOUR FEELINGS – CONSIDER YOUR EMOTIONS. THROUGHOUT THE DAY ASK YOURSELF, 'WHAT DO I REALLY FEEL?'
- YOUR BEHAVIOUR – CHECK YOUR ACTIONS. ARE THEY IN LINE WITH YOUR THOUGHTS AND FEELINGS? IN OTHER WORDS, ARE YOU DOING WHAT YOU REALLY WANT TO DO?

---

business and I was absorbed with childcare. We lived above the shop, and I became more and more resentful of the beautiful furniture that seemed to be coming between my husband and me. Instead of expressing my feelings and putting our relationship first, I withdrew from him, and so he withdrew from me. It just got worse and worse until in the end I left. It was only after I had gone that I realised that he had been having an affair for the last few months. I was furious, disempowered and righteously indignant. If it was 'all his fault', I could feel exonerated.

A few years later, when I was feeling very much better about myself, I began to see how I had let myself become a victim in my first marriage. Instead of taking positive steps to try to make the relationship work when it had faltered, I had just blamed and cried, swinging from aggressive to submissive behaviour and back again. If I had used an assertive approach, the story might have been different.

By the time I met Richard, both he and I had been through plenty of relationship disasters; we both knew exactly what we didn't want from a love partnership. I had found my feet as an independent single mother, and he was working as a counsellor and management trainer. This time round I was confident enough to get involved in his life rather than to be threatened by it, and he in turn was interested in me. We started to work together in the business and in bringing up the children, and this mutual dedication has led to a brilliant marriage. But we have often said that if we had met while we were both acting as love victims, our relationship would never have worked. It takes two people who have the self-confidence to behave assertively to create a good, strong and enduring love partnership.

Six simple ways to take charge of your love life

1 Tell him what you want. Why do we often find this so difficult? Time and again we feel let down by men who don't come through for us. But how can we expect them to be able to anticipate our needs and wishes when experience has taught us all that men are definitely not telepathic? They *cannot read our minds*, and I think we should actually be grateful for this (do you *really* want him to know what you are thinking?). So appreciate your mental privacy and start to make your wishes clear, using diplomacy, tact and assertive behaviour skills. If you know what it is you want and can communicate this in a creative way, you are more than likely to get it.

2 Don't be a doormat. Love victims usually suffer from being people pleasers in all areas of their life as well as their love life. Love magnets, on the other hand, never let themselves be put upon. Check your answers to the following questions:

- Do you ever feel taken for granted?
- Do you ever ask permission to speak or to act in a certain way?

- Do you often use the word 'sorry'?
- Are you ever worried about what others are thinking?
- Do you ever think that people are 'better' than you?
- Is it hard for you to say no to people?
- Do you often find yourself doing things that you really don't want to do?
- Do you ever not say what you really mean?
- Do you often apologise for your behaviour?

Are you perhaps being too nice for your own good? If so, get a grip on your life and get ready to put your needs first. Remember that if you are over-concerned with pleasing others, you will never get what you really want. And if your objective is just to please your man, then think again. It takes two happy people to create a loving relationship; don't ever forget that your first goal is to please yourself.

3 Get intimate. Have you ever had so much to do that you couldn't spare the time to be close to your loved one? Life can be very busy, but beware that you are not using excessive busyness to hide a fear of intimacy. Sometimes when we are facing an emotional problem we find great relief in 'losing ourselves' in doing something, and this often helps us to sort things out. But if we keep filling up our time with a whirlwind of frantic activity, we create an impenetrable boundary that stops others being able to reach us. Slow down and take the time that your love relationship deserves. Get in touch with your emotions and express them. Disclose your real feelings to your lover and let him express his. Nurture your love relationship and water it with intimacy or it will die of neglect.

4 Don't give up on love. The more you think about something, the bigger it gets, so stop obsessing about your inadequacies and generate self-belief instead. Self-doubt is the biggest obstacle you will ever encounter in life, and it will certainly stop you moving forward to achieve your potential. You can do whatever it is you think you can do, and this includes having a great love relationship. So, you have made some poor love choices in the past, you have acted like a love victim, you have been disappointed and felt heartbroken . . . Well, haven't we all? These are not good reasons to give up on love! Get smart and let your relationship history work for you. Recognise what went wrong and why, and resolve never to make the same mistake again.

5 Be a winner. Love victims create scenarios in which they always lose, whereas love magnets create winning situations. One fabulous way to improve your relationship 100 per cent is to use the following technique. Whenever you are in conflict with your loved one try *putting yourself in his shoes*.

- Before you dive in there, take a deep breath and count to ten (at least!).
- Turn your focus away from the conflict and try to understand where he is coming from.

- Let him have his say and he will be more ready to listen to you.
- Don't jump to conclusions or prejudge him.
- Ask questions so that you gain useful information.
- Listen to his answers.
- Treat him respectfully.

Now you will have a new way of looking at the situation. Can you understand it from his point of view? From his vantage point can you see a result that would be a win for you and for him? If so, act on this. And if he cannot respond well to this assertive approach, ask yourself, 'Is he a love victim?' If he is a loser in the game of love, at least you have found this out.

6 Attract positive and sensitive men. Yes, there are some out there, but you will only get their attention if you are giving out the right messages. If a man is self-confident and knows his own mind, he is a love magnet who will be looking for another love magnet; he will not be interested in a love victim. So get a life and then get a man. Great men want to be with women who they can trust and respect, so cultivate those qualities in yourself. Remember that whatever energy you give out will be reflected back to you in some way. Be assertive, go for your goals, get focused and generate bags of enthusiasm for life and you will open the door to some similarly motivated men!

MEDITATION MOMENT

THE WORLD HEART EMBRACE

THIS GESTURE IN EXERCISE HAS BEEN DESCRIBED AS THE MOST LIFE-AFFIRMING; IT IS THE PRIMAL LOVING WELCOME OF THE ETERNAL MOTHER. MUSCLE TESTING SHOWS THAT MERELY SEEING THIS GESTURE WILL STRENGTHEN THE LIFE FORCE.

- STAND UP AND REALLY STRETCH.
- NOW INHALE DEEPLY AND HOLD OUT YOUR ARMS AS WIDE AS YOU CAN. IMAGINE THAT YOU ARE EMBRACING THE WHOLE WORLD.
- HOLD THE STRETCH AND THE VISION FOR AS LONG AS YOU CAN HOLD YOUR BREATH.
- AS YOU EXHALE, BRING YOUR ARMS SLOWLY, GENTLY AND LOVINGLY TOGETHER SO THAT YOUR HANDS FOLD OVER EACH OTHER ON YOUR CHEST.
- YOU HAVE BROUGHT THE LOVE OF THE WHOLE WORLD INTO YOUR HEART. FEEL IT ENTER EVERY PART OF YOUR BODY.
- SPEND A FEW MOMENTS APPRECIATING THE FEELING OF WARMTH AND WELLBEING.
- REPEAT THESE ACTIONS AGAIN. KNOW THAT AS YOU INHALE AND STRETCH, YOU ARE SENDING OUT LOVE TO THE UNIVERSE, AND AS YOU EXHALE AND BRING YOUR HANDS TO YOUR CHEST, YOU ARE RECEIVING THE LOVE OF THE WORLD.

THE UNIVERSAL LIFE FORCE FLOWS THROUGH US CONTINUALLY. THIS BEAUTIFUL EXERCISE HELPS US TO BECOME AWARE OF THE LOVE INSIDE US AND AROUND US. START TO TAP INTO THIS LOVE AND YOU WILL BEGIN TO FEEL ITS AMAZING EFFECTS IN ALL PARTS OF YOUR LIFE. THE MORE LOVE YOU RADIATE, THE MORE YOU WILL ATTRACT. LOOK FOR LOVE AND YOU WILL SEE IT EVERYWHERE.

Step 5
Be a Sex Goddess

Nearly a third of all households in the UK reputedly own a vibrator. This makes them more common than cats.

TRACEY COX

What exactly are the credentials of a *bona fide* sex goddess? Of course, your thoughts immediately turn to such gorgeous creatures as Marilyn, Madonna and Nigella (Lawson) and will no doubt include other glamorous celebrity icons whose glitzy images adorn the media. But let's just stop star-gazing for one moment and consider reality. Who do you know who acts like a sex goddess? You know who it is I am talking about; she's that maddening girl who always looks downright sexy, even wearing jeans, no make-up and last season's haircut. In fact it's probably her very lack of contrivance that gives her that super-magnetic quality. Isn't it infuriating how she always manages to attract attention even when she is totally unaware of it? How does she do it? What has she got? And how can you get some?

Well, I can tell you what she's got; she's got her own unique style and she is just being herself. The truth is that you will never find your own inner sex diva while you are trying to reach the (impossible) dizzy heights of celluloid and airbrushed physical perfection. A real sex goddess *never* compares herself with others; she is at home in her own skin and she is in touch with her sensual side. Her positive attitude gives her body confidence and sex-esteem, and these two qualities mean that she acknowledges her own needs (sexual and otherwise) and expects to satisfy them.

And isn't that why we all loved Carrie, Miranda, Samantha and Charlotte so much? *Sex and the City* was one of the most successful TV sitcoms in history because for the first time we heard modern, fashionable women talk freely and humorously about their own sexual needs and desires. Yes, I know these girls were also impossibly successful/glamorous/intelligent, etc., but we were still able to recognise something of ourselves in them. They were great friends who shared their sexploits, and they knew how to have fun with or without a man! Even when their relationships were in the pits they refused to become love victims like Ally McBeal and Bridget Jones. No, our four heroines lived like love magnets whose spirits could always be revived by a new pair of Manolo Blahnik heels from Bergdorfs or Saks, or perhaps by a vibrator!

When prudish Charlotte falls in love with her Rampant Rabbit she even loses the will to date! This episode led to an amazing rush of women to their nearest Ann Summers outlet, and figures show that now one woman in three owns a vibrator (so they really *are* more common than cats!). Sex toys have become acceptable. At last we are recognising our own sexual needs.

Enter the sex goddess!

Yes, the sex goddess is a real woman who loves her own sexuality and knows what turns her on and off. She lives a busy life, juggling home, career and possibly a partner and children, and she is usually exhausted by the end of the day. So how does she keep radiating sexuality and glamour? How does she arrive home from work full of zest and vitality ready for a steamy night of passion with her loved one? *How on earth does she do it?*

Relax, she doesn't. A recent survey reveals that three out of five women would rather soak in a bath than have sex. Forty-two per cent would rather go shopping and

more than 50 per cent would rather watch a film with a box of chocolates. Let these figures put you at your ease. If you are not indulging in hot passionate sex within the next ten minutes, you are definitely in the majority.

Sex-esteem and body confidence

Zena, 48, is a university lecturer and she plays in a band. We go back a long way, to the time when we were both single mothers, in our early thirties. She was always brilliantly talented – played guitar, sang like a bird and was a forceful and flamboyant character. Zena always seemed larger than life. She was unusual, appeared confident and was determined to do her own thing come what may. She was a free spirit, and I admired her emotional independence and strength of character. But over the years Zena has lurched from one short disastrous love affair to another, and I have watched her gradually losing her old sparkle and zest for life.

Even in the old days Zena did have one major hang-up: she hated her large breasts and always wore baggy tops to keep them hidden. She never discussed her body image, and I had no idea how much her lack of body confidence had affected her relationships over the years. About five years ago she met a lovely man called Tim (also into music) and she is now very happy with him. Only recently did she reveal to me how her lack of body confidence had almost ruined her chances of ever falling in love. Every one of her relationships had been a sexual failure because she just couldn't feel relaxed and at ease with her body. Her lack of sex-esteem had escalated until she began to hate the thought of sex so much that she stopped having intimate relationships. Zena says now that her lack of body confidence dominated her life for all those years: she would never go on a beach holiday, or wear T-shirts or fitted clothes, or make love with the light on, or even allow herself to be seen naked by a lover. She says that she 'wasted her youth' worrying about her body shape, and it's only now, in middle age, that she can at last let go of her preoccupation.

So what happened to Zena to give her back her sex-esteem? Well, nothing specific except that she really loved Tim and knew that he loved her for who she was, and she didn't want to lose him. Getting older had also helped her to face her inhibitions, and she had at last stopped continually comparing herself physically with other women. She says, 'I guess I just got happy with myself, *all parts* of myself, and my big breasts didn't seem to matter any more. Life is too short to spend obsessing about how you look, and I know that now.'

Are you struggling to love *all parts* of yourself? What happens when you look in the mirror? Do you see your inner radiance shining through or are you too busily preoccupied with your weight, hair, wrinkles, cellulite, etc., etc. When you look at yourself are you full of self-criticism? Let me tell you right now, this is not the way to go. This is not the way to become a sex goddess!

The majority of us struggle with our body image on a day-to-day basis. A recent survey shows that most of us are suffering from the so-called Bridget Jones syndrome. The symptoms include a drastic lack of body confidence and a total preoccupation with the way we look. A staggering 90 per cent of the 5,000 women surveyed admitted that the appearance of their body depressed them, and one in ten admitted to being on a 'constant' diet.

EXERCISE:

How body confident are you?

Choose answers A, B or C to discover how body confident you are.

Score 4 for each A
Score 2 for each B
Score 0 for each C

1 A man compliments your appearance.
A You thank him gracefully and feel good about yourself.
B You feel a bit embarrassed.
C You don't believe him and say something that puts you down.

2 You stand naked in front of a full-length mirror.
A You are able to view yourself objectively and see your strong points as well as your weaknesses.
B You can only see the parts of your body that you dislike.
C You would *never* stand naked in front of a mirror.

3 How often do you weigh yourself?

A Occasionally.

B A few times a week.

C Daily.

4 When you see pictures of gorgeous models or celebrities do you:

A Enjoy them for what they are.

B Wish that you looked like them and start to feel a bit inadequate.

C Immediately feel inferior and not good enough.

5 Name three things that you love about your physical appearance.

A This was easy to do.

B It wasn't easy but you did it.

C You found this impossible to do and you felt depressed.

6 You are going out to buy a new outfit.

A You are delighted; you love clothes shopping.

B It's not your favourite thing because you feel too self-conscious.

C You don't want to go, clothes shopping always feels humiliating.

7 It's a bad hair day.

A You soon forget about it and get on with your life.

B You keep looking in the mirror and try different styling products to get it under control.

C Your whole day is absolutely ruined.

8 If you lost weight you would feel:

A Pleased but you are not that bothered.

B Wonderful; it would be a great confidence boost.

C Happy at last. If you could only be thinner you know that your life would change.

9 Your age is beginning to show.

A You feel philosophical; you are bound to get wrinkles sometime.

B You often worry about ageing and you put a lot of effort into looking good.

C You are very afraid of losing your looks and think this means that you won't be loveable any more. You are always trying new procedures and products.

10 How would you describe your self-image?

A I feel good about myself.

B I sometimes feel negative about the way I look and feel.

C I don't feel at all happy with myself; my self-image is poor.

If you scored 0–8

Your body confidence is at rock bottom. You have lost sight of the real you. She is worth so much more than you are giving her credit for. It's time to get things in perspective or you will never have the sex-esteem you need to feel fabulous about yourself. Take heart. You are an amazing woman. Stop your superficial judgements.

If you scored 10–18

The good news is that you are able to appreciate your finer points, and this can eventually lead to real body confidence. As you become more and more positive about yourself, you will be able to allow yourself to be less than perfect. Concentrate on your positive aspects and you will begin to value yourself increasingly. Remember that you are good enough just the way you are.

If you scored 20–28

You can sometimes feel quite good about yourself, although you still have a self-critical streak. When you look in the mirror, try to see beyond your physical image to the warm, creative and exciting woman inside. Once you learn to love yourself (warts and all) your sex-esteem will go through the roof.

If you scored 30–40

Congratulations! You are strongly body confident, and this shows in the way you walk, talk and relate to others. You are positively upbeat most of the time and are not overly concerned with what other people think of you. You are your own woman and you are high in sex-esteem.

Strut your stuff

We all want the best for ourselves, and of course we all want to look and feel as good as we can. To achieve any goal, we need to be motivated, focused and realistic; these are the strategies of the go-getter. Apply these same techniques to stopping yourself being victimised by impossible and unreasonable self-expectations. For example, if you are constantly comparing yourself with young models, you will never be able to be happy with your own body. Make peace with yourself by recognising what you can change and what you can't. If you are small and curvy, you will never ever be tall and skinny. Don't waste your energy wishing for the impossible or you will always be disappointed with yourself. Get going on what you can change and accept and let go of what you can't.

And do bear in mind that looking and feeling sexy is not about looking perfect. The sexiest woman in the room is the one who feels good about herself *on the inside*. So stop chasing that 'perfect' body or face and start to show off your own original and remarkable self. *Get out there and strut your stuff!*

Always be a first-rate version of yourself

Whenever you are feeling low in the attraction stakes and wondering if you will ever feel gorgeous and sexy again, just take this brilliant tip from Judy Garland, who said, 'Always be a first-rate version of yourself, instead of a second-rate version of somebody else.' Although you will

INSTANT TIP

LOOK BEYOND YOUR IMAGE

STAND CLOTHED IN FRONT OF A FULL-LENGTH MIRROR AND TAKE A GOOD LOOK AT WHAT YOU SEE.

- SMILE AT YOURSELF AND IMAGINE THAT YOU ARE SEEING YOUR IMAGE FOR THE FIRST TIME.
- NOTICE HOW FRIENDLY AND ACCEPTING YOU LOOK.
- CHOOSE THE ONE THING YOU MOST LIKE ABOUT YOUR PHYSICAL APPEARANCE – HAIR, NAILS, SKIN, BOTTOM, ARMS . . . WHATEVER – AND ADMIRE IT. FLAUNT IT IN FRONT OF THE MIRROR.
- NOW BE PROVOCATIVE. FLIRT WITH YOUR IMAGE. YES, YOU CAN DO THIS. THERE'S NO ONE WATCHING, AND IT WILL MAKE YOU FEEL SEXY AND GLAMOROUS.
- LOOK INTO YOURSELF AND SEE YOUR STRENGTHS. FOCUS ON WHAT YOU KNOW YOU ARE GOOD AT AND YOU WILL SEE A WOMAN WHO YOU CAN ADMIRE LOOKING BACK AT YOU FROM THE GLASS.
- SAY TO YOURSELF, 'I LOVE YOU FOR WHO YOU REALLY ARE.'
- SPEND A FEW QUIET MOMENTS ADMIRING THIS TERRIFIC SEX GODDESS.

probably make a very poor imitation of J Lo, Madonna or Britney, you can make a fabulous version of the real, authentic and original you!

When you are at ease with yourself, that air of confidence just surrounds you and is one of the biggest turn-ons around; you are looking good and feeling good and it shows! A self-assured woman who is doing her own thing and not trying to impress is always attractive (regardless of her weight, shape or size of nose). Think of the sassy and charismatic Dawn French, who oozes sexuality and allure. In an age in which success is often equated with slimness, she might seem an unlikely role model, but Dawn has just been voted the personality who has most inspired Britain's younger women. Dawn (a size 20) has sex appeal in truckloads, and it has absolutely nothing to do with physical perfection and everything to do with her originality, personality and talent. She is purely and simply a first-rate version of herself.

Everyone can find fault with their body. This might be hard to believe, but it's true. Every day I hear from clients who are dissatisfied with what nature has given them: Alpha women who can't bear the size of their hips or thighs, or think their breasts are too small or too large; and high-powered men who are insecure about their paunch, receding hairline or lack of six-pack . . . and so it goes on. *Sexual confidence does not depend on how you think you look on the outside but rather on how you feel about yourself on the inside.* When you are feeling sexy, you look sexy. It's as simple as that.

Feeling sexy and looking sexy

Maintain a good body image by following this easy six-step plan.

Step 1 Learn to be grateful for your body, whatever its shape or size. This is the most important step; without this basic appreciation you will never be satisfied with yourself. Confidence is sexy, so watch your posture, lift your head and walk with pride. You are worth it!

Step 2 Make a list of your best features and emphasise them. If your legs are shapely, show them off! If your hands are beautiful, have a regular manicure. Loving your body makes you feel gorgeous.

Step 3 Take good care of your hair and make sure that you regularly have a really good cut. The state of our hair has a dramatic effect on the way we feel about ourselves (you don't need me to tell you this).

Step 4 Repeat the following mantra as you go about your daily life:

I love my body.

Keep saying this to yourself. Sing it in the car, in the shower; write it on a piece of paper and stick it on the wall. You may find this step difficult, especially on a low day: say it even more on a low day; that's when you need it most. Surround yourself with positive thoughts about your body and soon you will believe them! Loving your body gives you a sexy glow.

Step 5 Use your favourite beauty products to make you feel really special. Take time out to pamper yourself and have a health farm extravaganza in the privacy of your own home. Indulge yourself and you will feel sensuous and sexy. Or alternatively splash out on a professional massage, facial or whatever you fancy – sheer bliss and a very worthwhile investment (you will feel like a million dollars).

Step 6 Throw out all those clothes that don't suit you. Only wear something that is really you; don't ever buy something just because it's fashionable. Develop a signature style that expresses who you are. Be brave, bold and adventurous here. If you really haven't a clue, it might be worth investing in a session with a stylist, or you could ask a personal shopper or an elegant friend for advice. Wearing your clothes well, with a relaxed look, shows that you are at home in your body and that you are sexually confident. As the ultra-chic Coco Chanel once famously said, 'Adornment is never anything but a reflection of the self.' Let your clothes reflect your fabulous, gorgeous self!

Respect and love your body enough to make the very best of yourself. You know that you are worth this attention, and it will make you feel terrific. Have you noticed that when you are feeling good about yourself, you attract other people to you? When you love yourself, others will love you too.

INSTANT TIP

GET THINGS IN PERSPECTIVE

A SEX GODDESS KNOWS THERE IS MUCH MORE TO LIFE THAN WORRYING ABOUT HER SAGGING BODY PARTS, BROKEN NAILS AND CELLULITE. SHE KNOWS THAT LIFE IS FOR LIVING AND SHE WILL NOT MISS A PRECIOUS MOMENT GETTING DEPRESSED ABOUT MINUTIAE.

SO ON A BAD HAIR DAY (OR BAD WHATEVER DAY) JUST UPLIFT YOURSELF AND TAKE A BIGGER PERSPECTIVE ON LIFE. RATHER THAN ASKING, 'WHY DO I LOOK SO FAT?', YOU COULD ASK, 'WHAT IS THE MEANING OF MY LIFE?' PUT THE FOCUS OF YOUR ATTENTION WHERE IT WILL BRING POSITIVE LIFE-AFFIRMING RESULTS. GET THINGS BACK INTO PERSPECTIVE BY ANSWERING THE FOLLOWING QUESTIONS.

- WHO ARE THE PEOPLE YOU LOVE MOST IN THE WORLD?
- WHAT QUALITY DO YOU MOST ADMIRE IN YOURSELF?
- IF YOU HAD ONLY ONE WEEK TO LIVE, WHAT WOULD YOU SAY TO WHOM?
- WHAT WOULD YOU LOVE TO ACCOMPLISH?
- ARE YOU AFRAID TO TAKE CHANCES? IF SO, WHY?
- WHAT VALUES ARE MOST IMPORTANT TO YOU?
- DO YOU BELIEVE IN YOURSELF?
- WHAT IS YOUR MOST WONDERFUL ACHIEVEMENT?

- DO YOU LOVE LIFE?
- WHAT HOLDS YOU BACK?

WHENEVER YOU LOSE TOUCH WITH YOUR INNER SEX DIVA, IT MEANS THAT YOU HAVE STOPPED APPRECIATING YOUR BODY, YOUR MIND, YOUR FEELINGS AND YOUR LIFE.

WHENEVER YOU LOSE YOUR SPARKLE, JUST THINK ABOUT YOUR ANSWERS TO THESE QUESTIONS. YOU HAVE COME TO THIS WORLD TO MAKE YOUR OWN SPECIAL CONTRIBUTION, AND IT HAS ABSOLUTELY NOTHING TO DO WITH THE WAY YOU LOOK.

ALWAYS REMEMBER THAT THE QUALITY OF YOUR LIFE DEPENDS UPON THE WAY THAT YOU LIVE IT. REACH FOR YOUR BEST IN ALL THINGS AND DON'T LET YOURSELF GET LOST IN SUPERFICIALITIES.

Sex, food and emotions

Comedienne Jo Brand jokes, 'My favourite sexual fantasy is smearing my naked body with chocolate and cream – then being left alone to lick it off.' Both sex and food feed our emotions and our appetites, because these four things are intricately connected. On a bad day, when we are comfort eating and feeling unhappy, our sex drive falls through the floor. This can become a vicious cycle as we start to feel even worse about ourselves. How on earth can we compete with these (airbrushed) images of stunning, confident and ravishing long-legged, perfect-bodied models? Sex sells, and we are surrounded by it on the streets, on buses, on trains and everywhere we look. And then, when we get home and put our feet up, there it is again, in books, magazines, TV, films . . . It's only too easy to feel pressurised by all the hype. We are led to believe that we are not fully functioning women unless we are having sex at least twice a day in a wide variety of positions, as well as achieving multiple orgasms.

You *know* it's all hype, so don't buy into it. You can enjoy the fashionable media glitz as long as you remember that it's all superficial; if you take it too seriously you will lose your own original and alluring sparkle. The pressure is on to be a sex siren with a perfect figure – an impossible goal for most of us, even without all our other daily demands. Small wonder then that we are driven to comfort eating and other sensual delights (other than sex, that is). Research demonstrates again and again that when we are low in body confidence, our sex drive falls and we are unhappy with our weight.

So how can you reach sex goddess status on a day when you feel fat, crave chocolate and are depressed by your body image? It's easy. You can break this negative cycle with positive action. Food and sex are good for you. Yes, if you increase the quality (not necessarily the quantity) of your food and zap up your sex life, you will feel revitalised.

Eat lots of fresh fruit and vegetables, as these are full of the minerals and vitamins needed to produce sex hormones. Substitute bananas for chocolate. Bananas are high in bufotenine, a chemical that induces confidence, happiness and (possibly) sex drive. Recent research in American shows that a low-fat high-protein diet can improve sex drive in a few weeks, so all the more reason to ditch the biscuits.

And even if you are not feeling at your vibrant best, just think of the following added benefits that sex brings. The average lovemaking session burns off about 200 calories and helps to tone your body. Sex is relaxing and mood-boosting, because it stimulates the production of endorphins (pleasure hormones) which reduce stress. And, perhaps even more importantly, you will have coaxed your inner sex diva out of hiding and she will make you feel reborn!

So next time you get the blues, forget the comfort eating (the 'comfort' is only very short-lived) and face your emotions head on. Be assertive and take control of your mood and you will start to feel better right away. Remind yourself that cake and crisps won't do it for you but increased energy levels and libido will.

Get those sexy hormones soaring

According to Sophia Loren (who ought to know), 'Sex appeal is 50 per cent what you've got and 50 per cent what people think you've got.' Inner confidence, body confidence and sex-esteem are all connected. When we are happy in our own skin we are more at ease with who we are and can begin to accept the way we look (wobbly bits and all). It isn't always easy to love and accept ourselves, but if we learn how to get in touch with our sensual and erotic side we will open a portal to great pleasure and satisfaction. Don't be shy about your sexual desires; don't let your inhibitions rob you of a full and satisfying sex life. There is plenty of great female erotica to be found in any high street book shop, so why not treat yourself and start to indulge in your own fantasies (you will be amazed and delighted by how this will make you feel).

One of the biggest sexual differences between men and women (excluding the obvious ones) is the amount of time each sex spends thinking about sex. If the figures are to be believed, men think about sex about once every two minutes – this means thirty times an hour! *Thinking about sex makes you feel sexy.* How many times an hour or a day or even a week do you think about sex? See, there's no comparison, is there? Most men, or so we're told, think about sex most of the time, and most women, apparently, don't. Here we can learn something to our advantage. *Start thinking about sex.* Begin immediately and you will find that this simple technique works wonders. The more you think about sex, the more sexual you will feel. Start to admire men's bodies, indulge in erotic fantasies and feel your libido soar!

Ten ways to release your inner sex goddess
1 Wear silk underwear (or no underwear). This will always add a dash to your day.
2 Indulge in long steamy fragrant baths (alone or accompanied).

3 Buy exotic perfume and lotions and potions.

4 Read female erotica.

5 Pamper your body and tend to it with loving care.

6 Read about sexual techniques and tips to create romance.

7 Think and talk about sex (to your friends).

8 Be romantic and sexually assertive.

9 Don't be afraid to try something imaginative and adventurous (sex toys, a new position, outdoor sex . . .).

10 Fantasise and get your juices going.

MEDITATION MOMENT

MEET YOUR INNER SEX DIVA

RELAX, CLOSE YOUR EYES AND LET GO OF ANY MENTAL OR PHYSICAL STRESS. IF THIS SEEMS IMPOSSIBLE, JUST ACKNOWLEDGE YOUR STRESS AND THEN IGNORE IT.

- IMAGINE A FABULOUSLY EXOTIC LOCATION – A HOT HAWAIIAN BEACH, A COOL MOUNTAIN RETREAT, AN UPBEAT AND HIP RESTAURANT, A LUXURIOUS SPA . . . CHOOSE WHATEVER TURNS YOU ON.

- VISUALISE YOURSELF IN YOUR CHOSEN SURROUNDINGS, LOOKING GOOD AND FEELING LANGUOROUS.

- SEE YOURSELF LOOKING RELAXED, CONFIDENT AND GORGEOUSLY SEXY.

- YOU KNOW YOU ARE LOOKING GOOD. GET INTO HOW THIS FEELS.
- NOTICE WHAT YOU ARE WEARING (IF ANYTHING).
- NOTICE YOUR POSTURE, YOUR HAIR, YOUR FACE. SEE YOUR INNER RADIANCE SHINING THROUGH.
- WATCH YOURSELF TALKING WITH OTHERS AND NOTICE THEIR ADMIRING GLANCES. YES, YOU ARE HOT!

YOU HAVE MET YOUR INNER SEX DIVA AND SHE IS ALL YOU COULD WISH FOR AND MORE. GET INTO HER SKIN, HAIR, FEELINGS, CONFIDENCE, SENSUALITY, POSTURE, SMILE AND EROTICISM. THIS IS A WOMAN WHO KNOWS HER SEXUAL NEEDS AND ISN'T AFRAID TO MEET THEM.

CAPTURE A COMPLETE IMAGE OF THIS LUSCIOUS, DELICIOUS CREATURE IN YOUR MIND. WHENEVER YOU NEED SOME RAZZMATAZZ, JUST STEP INTO HER PERSONA – SHE IS DYNAMITE!

Step 6
Get Him Talking

After the Martians learned how to listen they made the most amazing discovery. They began to realise that listening to a Venusian talk about problems could actually help them come out of their caves in the same way as watching the news on TV or reading a newspaper.

JOHN GRAY

John Gray's *Men Are from Mars, Women Are from Venus* must be the best-known relationship book ever written. Published in 1993, it became an instant international bestseller, taking a fresh and realistic look at the basic differences between men and women and offering ways to use this knowledge to improve our love lives. Some relationship experts have argued that the broad categorisation of women into Venusians and men into Martians is unhelpful as it reinforces the concept of irreconcilable gender differences, but I beg to differ.

My job as a life (and love) coach is to demonstrate how you can get the very best result for yourself in any situation. This will always mean knowing what you want, focusing on your goal, creating an action plan and gathering all the information and support that you need to help you achieve your outcome. We wouldn't dream of turning up for a job interview unprepared or of making any crucial decision without forethought, yet we quite happily go about 'falling' in and out of relationships without doing any preparatory groundwork. Don't think that being prepared for love will lessen the romance. The truth is that if you are unprepared *there will be no real romance*.

Let's just get one thing straight: men and women are different! And it's absolutely no good being aware of this fact unless you know exactly *how* these differences may manifest in your intimate relationships. When you are feeling severely irritated by your man and you mention his behaviour to women friends, they will raise their eyebrows and say, 'a typical man'. And although this female understanding and solidarity is an immediate comfort, it does nothing to help you to resolve your relationship issue.

Why does a 'typical man' expect a woman to think, communicate and react the way that he does? And why do we make the mistake of expecting men to feel, communicate and respond in the ways that we do? Knowledge is power, so let's use all the information we can gather to appreciate the different ways that men and women tick. When we remember that men are from Mars and women are from Venus, we can begin to understand what is really happening in our relationships.

What women really want

The founding father of psychoanalysis, Sigmund Freud, once admitted, 'The great question . . . which I have not been able to answer, despite my thirty years of research into the feminine soul, is "What does a woman want?"' Ask yourself. What single thing would most improve the quality of your life? Oh how the mind boggles with endless possibilities: fame, fortune, facelift, fulfilling career, fabulous sexy man . . . But a recent survey by a top women's magazine reveals that 60 per cent of women answering this question asked only *that their partner would spend just 15 minutes a day talking to them 'meaningfully'*. Sounds a modest enough request, doesn't it? However, you and I know that this is actually female code for what we *really* want, which is for men to talk to us about their feelings. And so this apparently simple wish actually opens a Pandora's box of relationship issues: men and women seem to come from different planets. We don't even speak the same language, so how can we possibly reconcile these differences and learn to communicate harmoniously?

When Pandora lifted the lid, all the ills of the world escaped from the box and there was only one thing left, lying at the bottom, and that was hope. And this is what we have when we lift the lid on our relationship issues: we can dare to look at what needs to change because we can be hopeful about the outcome. If we carry on expecting men to be like women, we will carry on being disappointed and let down by love. In life coaching we say that if you keep acting the same way you will get the same result; the only way to get a new outcome is to change your own behaviour. Now just apply this simple theory to your love life. You can always change a situation by changing your own approach. This is why you can be hopeful of getting what you want from a man.

Gemma, 29, is a jewellery designer. For two years she has been living with David, 28, a City insurance broker. Gemma told me that when they met they were enraptured by the differences between them but that they eventually lost this mutual adoration and became constantly angry and irritated with each other. From the moment I spoke to Gemma I felt optimistic about her outcome, because she never once blamed David and she could see that they didn't view their relationship in the same way – she was aware of their differences.

They met at a party in a fashionable art gallery and were immediately fascinated by each other's background and work. Gemma says, 'He was gorgeous, so reserved and polite, and looked very smart and a bit out of place amongst the pushy arty crowd. I'm into wearing vintage clothes and lots of my own jewellery, so from the start we looked like we came from different worlds. And at first this is what we most loved about each other. But David was always quite formal and precise in the way he talked, and I always felt that there was much more to him than he showed – and of course that was an exciting challenge to me. I am very emotional and I wear my heart on my sleeve, and at first he loved my outbursts and was always ready with a hanky and a shoulder to cry on.

Then we moved in together into his flat and things started to crack. He is neat and orderly, and I am a creative person who likes to be surrounded by my artistic bits and pieces and whatever ideas I am working on. David blew up one night and threw all my fashion magazines in the bin and coldly said that I had got to get myself more in order. I was devastated and told him that he would never understand where I was coming from because he was so prissy and uptight. From that moment we withdrew from each other and we were both hurting very much. I knew that we needed to open up the communication again, but David reacted by closing down emotionally and going to the gym every night.' It was at this point that Gemma contacted me.

She had a clear goal, and that was to get their relationship back on track. She felt that it was quite possible if only they could break their stalemate position and learn to trust each other again. Eventually they did resolve their issues, but this only happened when Gemma changed her behaviour. When we looked back at past instances when she and David had become locked in dispute, she could see that it was often precipitated either by her getting over-emotional or by David getting over-logical. In a relationship crisis, women's favourite fallback position is often a purely emotional one. And men are inclined to turn to a logical problem-solving mode in order to find their way out of their distress. These preferred positions drive the other partner crazy (red rags to both bulls), and so the misunderstandings escalate.

Gemma did something very simple but very profound

and turned her relationship completely around. She started to become aware of her emotional responses and saw how these were only ever a limited reaction. And then, because she wasn't endlessly talking and expressing her feelings any more, this created a space for David. When she stopped overloading him with her own feelings she found that David then came out of his 'cave' (where logic and reason prevailed) and stepped into the space she had created. By adding some new communication and listening skills to her repertoire Gemma was able to encourage David to discuss his feelings, and in so doing she found that she herself felt less needy and more confident and balanced.

There is no magic involved here, just an awareness of each other's energy and the need for both men and women to balance their emotional and logical sides. If you only operate at an emotional level, your man will be forced into the opposite role. Try a change of behaviour and see how this works.

Women and men are different

It won't surprise you to know that women speak on average 23,000 words a day while men speak 12,000. Some of us might even think that 12,000 is a rather optimistic figure. Further research has revealed that women are expert at using both sides of their brains at once. This means that we can express our emotions as we feel them. It's so easy for us: we can feel and talk at the same time. *But men can't do this!* This is a vital piece of

INSTANT TIP

BE A GOOD LISTENER

ONE OF THE BEST WAYS TO GET HIM TALKING IS TO
DEVELOP YOUR OWN LISTENING SKILLS. THE CHINESE
VERB 'TO LISTEN' IS COMPOSED OF THE FIVE
CHARACTERS MEANING: *EAR*, *YOU*, *EYES*, *UNDIVIDED
ATTENTION* AND *HEART*. THIS TRANSLATION SUGGESTS
THAT LISTENING IS MORE THAN JUST HEARING. WHEN
YOU LISTEN IN THE CHINESE SENSE YOU ARE LISTENING
WITH YOUR HEAD AND YOUR HEART, AND THIS CREATES
A FANTASTIC FEELING OF TRUST IN THE PERSON WHO IS
SPEAKING; IT ALSO MEANS THAT YOU GET TO UNDER-
STAND MUCH MORE OF WHAT THE OTHER PERSON IS
TRYING TO CONVEY. GOOD COMMUNICATION DEPENDS
ON GOOD LISTENING SKILLS, SO TRY OUT THE
FOLLOWING TECHNIQUES WHEN HE NEXT BEGINS TO
TALK.

- CONCENTRATE ON HIM.
- MAINTAIN EYE CONTACT AS MUCH AS POSSIBLE.
- LISTEN TO THE CONTENT OF WHAT IS BEING SAID
  (WHAT DOES HE REALLY MEAN?).
- WATCH HIS BODY LANGUAGE (WHAT CLUES CAN YOU
  PICK UP HERE?).
- DON'T INTERRUPT.
- LISTEN FOR THE THINGS NOT BEING SAID (IS HE

IMPLYING SOMETHING, IS HE BEATING ABOUT THE
BUSH, IS HE NOT SAYING WHAT HE MEANS?).

- KEEP AN OPEN MIND THROUGHOUT (AS SOON AS
  YOU START CREATING MENTAL JUDGEMENTS AND
  WORKING OUT YOUR RESPONSES YOU HAVE STOPPED
  REAL LISTENING).
- WATCH YOUR OWN BODY LANGUAGE. IS IT OPEN
  AND RECEPTIVE?

YOU WILL BE STAGGERED BY HOW DIFFERENT IT IS TO
CONCENTRATE ON LISTENING AS OPPOSED TO TALKING.
TRY A DAY OF LISTENING, IN WHICH YOU PRACTISE
THESE SKILLS WITH EVERYONE YOU MEET. YOU WILL
DISCOVER THAT THE WHOLE WORLD WANTS TO BE
LISTENED TO AND WILL LOVE YOU FOR YOUR
ATTENTION. LISTENERS ARE ALWAYS THE PEOPLE WHO
OTHERS TURN TO WHEN THEY WANT TO DISCUSS THEIR
EMOTIONS, SO GET PRACTISING AND ALLOW YOUR MAN
TO GET TALKING.

information to remember. Instead of talking about his
feelings, your man will channel his emotions into actions
(you know all about this). Don't automatically jump to the
conclusion that: he is not feeling anything, he does not
want to communicate his feelings, he would rather go out
with his mates than work things out with you, he can't be
bothered to put anything into your relationship, he

doesn't love you . . . need I go on? The next time you are revving up for a good row and he ups and leaves for a while, don't tear your hair out. Remember that *he cannot express what he is feeling at the moment* but that he will be able to later, when he has processed this emotional information. I know it's infuriating when he comes back and has forgotten all about the argument and you have spent all that time seething and stewing, but get wise to the differences between you. You are streets ahead in the emotional literacy skills department. Let this work to your advantage.

Women and men react totally differently to stress. Women are inclined to get more overwhelmed and emotionally involved and men tend to get more focused and withdrawn. This is what John Gray means when he says that in order to feel better 'Martians go to their caves to solve problems alone,' while 'Venusians get together and openly talk about their problems.' The basic difference appears to be that men feel better when they are either trying to solve dilemmas or trying to forget them, and women feel better when they are talking about their problems.

Consider the following scenario: John and Jane have both had a hard day at work and are feeling stretched. John wants to relax and forget his troubles by watching the news on TV. Jane also wants to unwind, but she can only start to feel better once she has talked about her day. Jane tries to talk and John tries to watch TV. He thinks that Jane talks too much, and she thinks that he is ignoring her.

The resolution of this situation doesn't depend on how much they love each other but on how much they appreciate their different needs. If Jane doesn't understand that John needs to withdraw into his mind (eg watch TV) in order to feel happier, she will feel ignored and hurt by him. And if John doesn't know that Jane needs to talk about her problems before she can feel better, he will carry on pulling away from her – while she carries on trying to make him respond even when he obviously doesn't want to.

Any man or woman who is unaware of the different ways that the opposite sex operates is heading for a relationship disaster. Look around you at the supermarket, in a restaurant, on holiday, and you can see couples misunderstanding and disagreeing with each other simply because they do not know that men and women *behave and communicate differently*. Successful love relationships depend upon both partners appreciating, respecting and enjoying their differences. If John had listened to Jane for ten minutes, she would have been quite happy to let him watch TV. And if Jane had let John unwind, he would then have been happy to listen to her. Use this important information about gender differences to oil the wheels of your relationship. Stop expecting the impossible and then you will not be disappointed.

Encouraging him to talk

You can get your man to talk, but you need to plan your approach.

- **Stop making confrontational statements.** Don't say things like: 'Why don't we talk to each other any more? You never tell me how you feel.' or even 'Why don't we plan some time to talk?' You will not get the desired results if he feels criticised by your suggestions. Try a more creative approach. For example you could say: 'I miss our great chats. Let's go for a drink and catch up with each other. I love it when you talk to me; you are such a great person to talk to.' Tell him the truth; show him how much you need and appreciate him, and he will respond beautifully.

- **Organize Talk Time.** Create some time in your busy schedules when you can be intimate and attentive. Be subtle, re-create your early dating days and give him your full attention (men love this). Ask him about his activities – this can lead to greater things. Don't expect too much at once.

- **Let him talk.** And once he starts chatting, *let him talk!* Resist all temptation to empathise with him. Women fall automatically into 'overlapping' mode when they talk to each other. Your friend discloses a problem and you say something like, 'I know exactly what you are going through.' We do this with each other to show support, and it brings us closer together. Beware, *men hate this* *technique.* Resist the temptation to jump in there or he will close up and it will be you who is doing all the talking (again). Learn to listen well and leave some spaces for him to talk into.

- **Remember that men and women communicate differently.** Men speak to give information, and women speak to create emotional bonds. Always keep this in mind.

Don't expect a man to do more than one thing at a time.

In their brilliant book, *Why Men Don't Listen and Women Can't Read Maps*, Barbara and Allen Pease write: 'Ask men and women if their brains work differently. Men will say they think they do; in fact there was something they were reading on the Internet the other day . . . . Women will say, of course they do – next question?' Barbara and Allan suggest that we try the Toothbrush Test. Because women can multi-task, they can brush their teeth, walk around and talk on a variety of topics *at the same time* (yes, I have done this, and I expect that you have too). Apparently we can also make up-and-down strokes with the toothbrush while simultaneously polishing a table with circular movements of the other hand! Most men, it seems, would find these clever tricks impossible because their mono-tracked brain means that they can only focus on one task at a time.

INSTANT TIP

KNOW WHEN IT'S NOT GOOD TO TALK

'IT'S GOOD TO TALK,' AS THE ADVERT SAYS, BUT SOMETIMES IT'S JUST NOT THE RIGHT TIME TO DO IT.

ALTHOUGH YOU MIGHT BE ANXIOUS TO HAVE YOUR SAY, OR CLEAR THE AIR, OR GET TO THE BOTTOM OF SOME IMPORTANT ISSUE, ALWAYS MAKE SURE YOU HAVE CHOSEN AN APPROPRIATE TIME. ONE THING THAT A LONG MARRIAGE HAS TAUGHT ME IS THE VALUE OF TIMING; IN FACT SOMETIMES A GOOD OUTCOME RELIES ENTIRELY ON PICKING YOUR MOMENT WITH CARE. SO GET THE TIMING RIGHT AND DON'T TRY TALKING WHEN:

- YOU ARE FEELING ANGRY AND OUT OF CONTROL. TEMPTING THOUGH IT MIGHT FEEL TO LET RIP, THIS IS NOT A GOOD TIME. WAIT UNTIL YOUR EMOTIONAL TEMPERATURE DROPS AND YOU WILL BE MUCH MORE LIKELY TO APPROACH THE SITUATION ASSERTIVELY.
- ONE OR OTHER OF YOU IS EXHAUSTED. OVER-TIREDNESS ALWAYS LEADS TO OVER-SENSITIVITY, SO TAKE THAT VERY GOOD IF RATHER OLD-FASHIONED ADVICE AND 'SLEEP ON IT'. THINGS MAY LOOK VERY DIFFERENT THE FOLLOWING MORNING.
- THERE IS AN IMMEDIATE CRISIS THAT NEEDS SORTING OUT. IF AN EMERGENCY DEVELOPS, SOMEONE NEEDS

So if he doesn't answer you when he is reading the paper or driving (or having sex!), it is because he really cannot concentrate on what you are saying. He's not being obtuse, uncaring, selfish or deliberately unkind; it is just all too much for him to cope with. Remember this the next time you feel ignored and unheard. Perhaps his mind was fully occupied with some other task.

It can be hard for us to appreciate the male mind, because we have the great advantage of being able to access both sides of our brain simultaneously with greater efficiency than men can. The left side of the human brain specialises in logic, analytical reasoning and thinking; it processes information in a linear way. The right side specialises in intuition, creativity and emotional responses; it can cope with many simultaneous inputs and processes in a non-linear way. Now imagine that you have a computer on each shoulder (your right and left brain) and that there is a cable running between the two. This cable is called the corpus callosum and comprises a bundle of nerve fibres. Research shows that women's brains have a thicker corpus callosum than men's, with up to 30 per cent more connections between left and right. This explains why you can cook dinner, listen to the TV and carry on a conversation while at the same time planning tomorrow's workload. We call it multi-tasking, and it's how we get so much done. Men's brains are much more compartmentalised. They can't jump from one side to the other and back again with such facility; they just haven't got enough connecting fibres in their corpus callosum! So now you can stop expecting the impossible and just be hugely grateful for your ability to do three things at the same time.

The Do's and Don'ts of getting a man to do what you want him to do

Do be brief and direct. So, for example, you say, 'Would you bring in the shopping?' rather than, 'The shopping is in the car.' Men do not react well to indirect statements, especially if they imply an expectation ('I did the shopping so it's your job to bring it in.')

Don't ever try to change him. Accept him for who he is and he will become more open and trusting of you. Men need to feel accepted. If he feels you are implying that he needs improving or changing in any way he will assume that you don't think that he is good enough. This will never lead to a happy outcome.

Do ask for support. Never present a problem and expect him to rally round. Don't say, 'The hinge has come off this door' but say, 'Would you fix the hinge on this door?' If you don't ask directly for support then you will probably not get it. He needs clear instructions.

Do get the words right. You might think that using 'could' or 'can' makes your request sound less demanding, but if you are actually using them instead of 'would' or 'will' they may be irritating to a man. If you say, 'Can you put the rubbish out?', he will probably think of course he *can* but the point is *will* he. Men hate indirect statements, so be simple and logical and ask direct, easy-to-understand questions.

Don't sound demanding. Demands make a man feel criticised. If you imply that he is not doing enough, he will be put off doing anything else at all.

Do show your appreciation for all that he does. This includes things that you haven't asked him to do (as well as things that you have). We all hate to be taken for granted and are much more inclined to give of ourselves if we feel valued, so appreciate him lots and lots!

Don't think that he should know what you want without you telling him. Most men are not very tuned in to their intuition, so don't stew with resentment when he doesn't pick up your need to be supported. If there is the slightest hint of resentment in your voice, you will not get what you want. Acknowledge that if you want anything doing *you will have to ask*, so just go ahead and ask effectively.

Do respect his deep desire to go into his 'cave' when he needs to unwind. The sooner he gets the stress out of his system, the sooner you will be able to engage with him in meaningful communication. He will love your non-critical acceptance of his need to withdraw sometimes and will then feel much more inclined to give you the support you need. This is called practising the 'give and take' of relationships.

Don't expect a great show of emotional solidarity. He would always rather talk about work, sport or gadgets than engage in a conversation about his or your feelings. Don't force him to do what he finds so difficult or he will become even more resistant. Stop overloading him with your own emotions and polish up your listening skills and eventually he will start to open up. Give him time and space – *quiet* time and space – and just be patient. It will be worth it.

Do ask him for his advice. Men love this! What does he think? What would he do in this situation? What would he say to this or that person? Remember that he is comfortable with direct questions and he will feel closer to you and more involved if you include him in this way. This is a great way to get a man talking and to create emotional intimacy between you. Oh, and make sure you thank him for his input.

Love means learning how to ask

Women need to feel heard and to be able to share their feelings, while men are often chary about being asked for their support. This is not because they can't be bothered or they don't care; it's simply because we often make the mistake of expecting the men in our lives to *know what we want* (a cuddle, sympathy, a listening ear . . .) and when they don't come up with the goods and try to find solutions instead, we feel let down and resentful. As a result, our man feels criticised and rejected. I hope that this chapter has made it clear why men don't and can't always respond in the way we would like them to. Love does not mean never having to ask; it means learning how to ask.

If you are not asking for support, your man will probably assume he is giving you enough. Get realistic, get practical and use some assertive communication skills and you will be thrilled with the outcome. Women are intuitively connected to the needs of others and give emotional support as soon as it's needed; don't expect men to act in the same way. Remember they are just not wired in the same way that we are; they can't make instantaneous instinctive judgements so stop expecting this. The only way you can get what you want from a man is to make your wishes clear to him. Spell it out in black and white and show how much you value his efforts. He will only be confused by mixed messages, and angered and belittled by criticism, so be diplomatic and straightforward and *show him how much you appreciate him*.

Although we are different in many ways, men and women have the same basic need: to be supported, valued and appreciated in a love relationship. If you want a loving man in your life, you will have to use all your wit, judgement, intuition, creativity and resourcefulness to get what you want. The physiological make-up of the female brain puts you well ahead of the game, so use your gifts to make assertive relationship choices and achieve your love goals!

MEDITATION MOMENT

THE MAN OF YOUR DREAMS

WHATEVER YOU REPEATEDLY 'SEE' IN YOUR MIND WILL COME TRUE FOR YOU IN SOME WAY. IF YOU ARE CONTINUALLY RUNNING A NEGATIVE MOVIE IN YOUR HEAD ABOUT YOUR LOVE LIFE, THEN NEGATIVITY IS WHAT YOU WILL KEEP ON ATTRACTING. RELAX, CLOSE YOUR EYES AND TRY THE FOLLOWING VISUALISATION.

- SWITCH YOUR CONSCIOUSNESS FROM PROBLEMS TO SOLUTIONS. RATHER THAN FOCUSING ON WHAT YOU DON'T LIKE ABOUT YOUR LOVE LIFE, START FOCUSING ON WHAT YOU WOULD LIKE.
- HOW WOULD YOUR DREAM MAN BEHAVE?
- IMAGINE HIM AND YOU TOGETHER. NOTICE HOW LOVING AND SUPPORTIVE HE IS.
- SEE HIM LISTENING TO YOU AND KNOW THAT HE IS VERY SENSITIVE AND THOUGHTFUL.
- IMAGINE WHAT IT WOULD FEEL LIKE TO BE TOTALLY LOVED, APPRECIATED AND DESIRED.
- GET RIGHT INTO THE SKIN OF A WOMAN WHO IS WELL-LOVED BY HER MAN. FEEL HOW FABULOUS THIS IS.
- YOU KNOW THAT THIS MAN IS YOUR KNIGHT IN SHINING ARMOUR, DEPENDABLE, TRUSTWORTHY AND RESPECTFUL.

- SEE THE TWO OF YOU STANDING SIDE BY SIDE IN LIFE. YOU ARE A GOOD MATCH AND YOU ARE BOTH COMMITTED TO YOUR RELATIONSHIP.
- REPEAT THIS VISION AS OFTEN AS POSSIBLE AND START TO DRAW THIS SUPPORTIVE RELATIONSHIP INTO YOUR LIFE. THIS IS WHAT YOU DESERVE!

Step 7
Flirt Your Way
to Success

*Our deepest fear is not that we are inadequate.
Our deepest fear is that we are powerful beyond
measure. It is our light, not our darkness, that
most frightens us. We ask ourselves: 'Who am I
to be brilliant, gorgeous, talented, fabulous?'
Actually, who are you not to be?*

MARIANNE WILLIAMSON

Yes, who are you not to be? You are amazing, and if you
don't believe that about yourself yet, it's time to do so
right now, before we go any further. When I tell you that
you are a divinely talented and magnificent creature, how
do you feel? Are you uncomfortable with this? Do you
disagree? Do you agree?

The lovely, curvaceous and gifted Kate Winslet says,
'I'm insecure; everyone is.' I can believe this, because
Kate is only being ultra-honest about the human
condition. We *all* struggle with self-doubt and self-
criticism, although we all seem to find it hard to believe
that we are not the only one. When I give talks or

workshops, people are always amazed to discover that we all share similar fears and personal insecurities: we all sometimes think that we are *not good enough*! Hold this thought and let it be a starting point for your new way of communicating with the world as you begin to flirt your way to success.

Flirt coach Peta Heskell explains that flirting isn't just a sexual come-on but an ability to make great connections with people and to enable them to feel at ease in your company. You can give no one a greater gift than your full admiring attention. Everybody loves this and will love you for giving it. Think of that man you know who could charm the birds right off the trees, or the woman who has only to step into a room for the atmosphere to lighten and brighten. What have these two people got in common (apart from their popularity of course)? Well, they are ace communicators. This is their strength, although like all true professionals they make their craft look very easy. They have fabulous social skills and everyone loves being around them as they radiate goodwill, bonhomie and great vibes. Have you ever wished you could be this relaxed and at ease with people? Well, you can be like this. There really is no need to be a shrinking violet any more. Take the positive, optimistic, upbeat and charming you out there and flirt your way to success in your life (and this includes your love life). The term 'flirting' comes from the old French word *fleurter*, which means 'to flower'. So why not use all the tricks you have learned so far in this book and open up and blossom? Become a natural flirt by using the following skills.

Ten ways to become a natural flirt

1 Use your instincts to tell you what makes others feel good.

Forget about how you are feeling and home in on the other person (this is a great way to overcome your own shyness and nerves). Think about what you could say so that he or she will relax. Be generous with your time and attention and you will be richly rewarded.

2 Be flexible and create a rapport with all types of people.

Sometimes we are inclined to stick to the same 'type' of girlfriends and boyfriends. Don't let yourself get trapped socially like this. Spread your net wide, keep open-minded and remember that the perfect love for you might be someone you have never previously considered. Give everyone a chance to shine.

3 Become aware of your own sexuality and the power that it generates.

Get in touch with your inner sex goddess and be aware of her when you are with a potential love interest. Is there any sexual chemistry here? How does it feel? Would you like to take this further or not?

4 Keep the atmosphere light and positive – have fun!

When you make someone laugh, they automatically feel more relaxed and open. A recent *Cosmo* survey of 1,000 men showed that the qualities they most valued in a partner were not great looks and hot sex but fidelity, friendship and a good sense of humour. As it's also been scientifically proven that we are more attracted to people who make us smile, the message is simple – get light and laughing! The added bonus is that you will feel great however anyone else reacts.

5 Get out and meet people, network and create a social diary.

Shrinking violets never win the prizes in life. Make the effort to expand your social horizons and engagements. A full social life is a great thing whether you are with or without a man. And if you are looking for a love interest, you will have a far greater choice if you are out and about (don't expect him to come knocking on your door).

6 Be inspired by others; admire them for their strengths and good qualities.

When you focus on the positive rather than the negative aspects of people, you are reinforcing their own self-belief, and this makes them feel great. See the bigger picture in life and keep things in perspective. Remember it is *who* you are and not *what* you are that matters. Value people for what really counts and they will love you for it.

7 Use positive body language to show your interest in another person.

Make good eye contact and adopt a relaxed posture. This will have an immediate calming effect on the person you are talking to. If you are flirting with an eye to catching the attention of a potential love interest, there are some specific body signals you can send which we shall look at in detail later (see page 140).

8 Listen well.

Simple though it sounds, this is a hot flirting tip. Attention is sexy. There is no doubt that both men and women are attracted to a person who has time and attention for them. Natural flirts know how to listen with their whole self. This is such an uncommon quality that you will shoot into the natural flirting zone as soon as you begin to use it. Start practising immediately, and just watch the reaction.

9 If you are flirting in a sexual context then get a sense of when it's OK to take it further and when it's time to stop.

It's most important to know how far to go – don't be too pushy and back off if he is not interested. If he's interested you will know (we do, don't we), and then you can take it to the next deliciously exciting stage. If the signs are not promising, just let it go and remember you can't please all of the people all of the time. Don't waste time feeling rejected. Natural flirts know how to bounce back and move on.

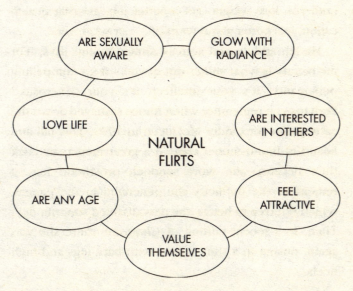

10 Have a love affair with life.

Natural flirts don't depend on others to make them feel good about themselves. They love their life and they create their own good times, and this is very attractive to others. When you give off that inner glow of confidence, you can really start to flirt with your life and have a wonderful time. Believe that you are sexy and attractive and you will automatically act as if you are!

Get over yourself and get going

There are no excuses for you; there is absolutely nothing to stop you becoming that charismatic and confident girl who is happy to take centre stage in life and love. Or is there? Perhaps you think you can't be like this until you change something about yourself. Is your life on hold until you lose weight, get a better job, get that qualification, feel better about yourself . . . or whatever?

Model, athlete and actress Aimee Mullins says, 'For me beauty is what shines out of you – it's a compelling personality, it's your intellect, it's your generosity.' Perhaps you remember when Aimee sashayed down the catwalk for Alexander McQueen in 1998. This tall and beautiful blond model created a great media stir back then because she wore wooden prosthetic legs. I remember the publicity she generated in the papers, which referred to her as 'the new disabled supermodel'. Then, in a recent edition of *Glamour*, there she was again, posing in a slinky dress with bare legs and high heels.

Aimee's interview in *Glamour* makes great reading for any prospective flirts who are struggling with issues of body confidence. This is a girl who had both legs amputated below the knee when she was only a year old and was told that she might never be able to walk. What a terrible start in life. But isn't it interesting how different people react to challenges? In the interview, speaking of those who cannot accept themselves the way they are, she has simply this to say: 'Get over yourself.' What great advice for all of us on a 'bad hair day', or a 'fat day', or in fact on any old day. Her message is to get a grip, get things in proportion and not sell yourself short. You are much too wonderful to disrespect yourself in this way!

Aimee is a natural go-getter who was always determined to reach for her best and let nothing stand in her way. She has chosen to excel in areas that rely on physical strength and beauty: she has set sporting records at the Paralympics, she models and has just made her first film. Whenever a lack of body confidence lets you down and you allow your feelings of not being physically 'good enough' to hinder your life in any way, bear a thought for this gorgeous girl who wouldn't let a little thing like two amputations get in her way. Let her story be an inspiration to you. Face it: there are no excuses left for you to hide behind. Love your life, have fun and get out there and strut your own unique stuff! Life is too short to waste hiding in the wings. Step into the arena and start to live. Get over yourself and shine!

INSTANT TIP

GLOW WITH INNER CONFIDENCE

LET GO OF ALL LIMITING THOUGHTS ABOUT YOURSELF. THEY WILL ONLY BRING YOU DOWN. IT'S TIME FOR THE SEXY, ATTRACTIVE GORGEOUS YOU TO RADIATE AND GLOW WITH CONFIDENCE. WHAT MAKES YOU FEEL REALLY GREAT ABOUT YOURSELF? FINISH THE FOLLOWING STATEMENTS AND DISCOVER YOUR NATURAL, FLIRTATIOUS AND INSPIRED SELF.

- I FEEL ATTRACTIVE WHEN . . . .
- MY FINEST ASSET IS . . . .
- I AM PROUD OF MY . . . .
- I GIVE OF MY BEST WHEN . . . .
- I RISE TO MY CHALLENGES BY . . . .
- I FEEL EMPOWERED WHEN I . . . .
- MY GREATEST STRENGTHS ARE . . . .
- NOTHING CAN STAND IN MY WAY WHEN . . . .
  . . . .
- WHEN I LOOK IN THE MIRROR I MOST ADMIRE MY .
  . . . .
- I FEEL SEXY AND FLIRTY WHEN . . . .
- THE MOST AMAZING THING I HAVE EVER DONE IS .
  . . . .
- I LOVE IT WHEN . . . .
- I AM INSPIRED BY . . . .

Flirts wear purple!

You probably know Jenny Joseph's fantastic poem 'Warning'. Part of it goes:

When I am an old woman I shall wear purple
With a red hat which doesn't go, and doesn't suit me.
And I shall spend my pension on brandy . . .
. . . and say we've no money for butter . . .
But maybe I ought to practise a little now?
So people who know me are not shocked and surprised
When suddenly I am old, and start to wear purple.

(If you want to read the whole thing, just type 'I shall wear purple' into your Internet search engine.) The poem is funny, irreverent and utterly poignant. It reminds us not to waste a moment being something other than what we are and never to wait for 'permission' to be our unique and original self. The poem has struck such a chord with women that the phrase 'I shall wear purple' has become synonymous with 'I shall do my own thing'.

EXERCISE:

I shall wear purple

Ask yourself the following questions:

- What would 'wearing purple' mean for you?
- What are you not doing because it might not be seen as the right thing?

- Are you compromising yourself by trying to fit in with someone else's agenda?
- What price are you paying for not being true to yourself?

If you are holding back any part of yourself, you will be feeling the strain. This is no dress rehearsal; this is the real thing. You will never have this moment again. Love magnets, sex goddesses and natural flirts are determined to do whatever it takes to make the very most of their lives.

Think of three ways in which you could start to 'wear purple' (be your own utterly original self) and write them down in your journal.

- I could . . . .
- I could . . . .
- I could . . . .

Now do them. Natural flirts never wait for permission to be themselves!

The Calendar Girls

The naked ladies of the Rylstone Women's Institute (aka the Calendar Girls) caused a great stir in the late 1990s when they stripped off to add some spice to their WI charity calendar. They hit the headlines here and in the States and became so famous that they have been immortalised in the film *Calendar Girls*, starring Julie Walters and Helen Mirren.

There is something so healthy and empowering about a group of middle-aged Yorkshire women getting their kit off to raise money that no wonder the film was such a great success. This brilliant group of natural flirts flew in the face of popular myths concerning sex, age, body confidence and physical 'perfection', and the public and the media loved them for it. So here's yet another excuse we can't hide behind: age is no barrier to sexuality and flirtatiousness. Being a flirt is a state of mind and has nothing to do with our age.

And staying with this issue for a moment, we cannot possibly fail to appreciate the sheer sexiness of Helen Mirren, who has been a hot pin-up as well as a first-rate actress for over 35 years. She is a heart-warming and vital reminder to all middle-aged women everywhere. At close to 60 she is still winning major acting awards and is still talked about in terms of her sexuality. Helen has style, grace, wit, charm, humour and gives the impression of being *utterly her own woman*. There is nothing so sexy and flirtatious as a woman who is at ease with herself and her world.

Making the first move

If you are single and on the lookout for 'Mr Handsome Stranger' you really must read Leil Lowndes' brilliant book, *How to Make Anyone Fall in Love with You*; it's full of great tips and strategies for romantic flirts and it will keep you laughing from start to finish. Leil advises, 'Sisters, do not be hesitant about making the first move. If you need more courage, think of it this way. Female choice is an evolutionary mandate given to a woman so she may select the best mate and thus assure the survival of the species. You are merely fulfilling your instinctive destiny when you overtly lure Mr Handsome Stranger. Mother Nature would approve.' Let's look at some of Leil's suggestions for attracting that new man into your life.

Imagine that you spot a man you fancy at a party, in a restaurant, in a bar, at the gym . . . or wherever. What do you do next? Most likely you meet his eyes for a split second and then look away. If you are braver, you may smile and then look away (as you don't want to seem pushy). But if this is your whole strategy, you are unlikely to elicit a response. You must do more than this if you want it to go further: a single smile is not flirtatious enough! Don't worry about making the first move; research demonstrates that when men respond to women's non-verbal advances they actually think that they have taken the initiative. As Leil Lowndes so aptly puts it, the male ego is a wondrous thing! Let this work for you and use any of the following moves to get a man to notice you and to respond (while all the time thinking he has made all the running!).

Ten ways to make the first move

These methods were proven effective in a scientific investigation made by a researcher called Monica Moore, who was testing the theory that women made two-thirds of all approaches between the two sexes. She observed over 200 women at a party and recorded what is known as their 'non-verbal solicitation signals'. The women created an active response from a variety of moves. Here are ten of them that worked well. Give them a try.

1 Smile brightly at him.
2 Gaze fixedly at him.
3 Look at him while touching your hair.
4 Bump into him 'accidentally'.
5 Send him short, darting looks.
6 Ask him to help you with something.
7 Lick your lips whilst maintaining eye contact.
8 Nod your head at him.
9 Glance at him, toss your head and then look back.
10 Walk close to him with exaggerated hip movements.

If these flirting tips are just too embarrassing for words, remember that they are only ways to achieve your outcome. If your initial goal is to attract his attention, try one or more of these time-honoured techniques, known and used successfully by women through the ages, then, as soon as his attention is hooked, let him think that pursuing you was all his idea.

Guerrilla marketing tactics for the successful flirt

Rachel Greenwald has written a hugely successful relationship book called *The Program: Fifteen Steps to Finding a Husband after Thirty*. Her premise is that the important question is not 'Why are you still single?' but rather, 'What are you going to do about it?'. Her proactive approach to finding a partner is based on powerful marketing tactics that she learned at Harvard Business School. Although you might cringe at her cool and calculating strategies, there is good sense in using a logical campaign to achieve an outcome. If meeting someone for a long-term relationship is your goal, it is only sensible to follow a well-thought-out action plan.

In business, guerrilla marketing is a term used to describe the implementation of many small, unexpected and unusual tactics to reach the customer and make a sale. It is based on the idea that persistence and ingenuity can work better than just repeating the 'same old' marketing methods. Persistence and ingenuity in pursuit of goals are certainly necessary qualities that we recognise in life coaching and also, of course, in love coaching. Think of yourself as the brand you are marketing and get creative with your strategy.

To start with, transform your everyday habits. Get out of your personal rut-making routines and plan some changes. Take your outward-going natural flirting style to some new venues, and do this daily. Plan at least one new excursion for every day of next week. Go shopping at a different supermarket for a change; go to the gym at a different time, and get off that treadmill and start lifting weights (the weights area is where all the men congregate); have a coffee at Costa instead of Starbucks; go out with a new girlfriend (who will have a new set of social connections); buy that book you want in Waterstones instead of Smiths (and check out the music and sports section while you are there). *Make the effort* to change your habits. Let's face it, if you haven't met your lifelong partner doing what you are doing already, it must be time to do something different!

And then, when you *do* meet someone fanciable over the bookshelves (or wherever), you need a follow-up plan. Don't be too worried about your ice-breaker, because the words you use will not be significant. If a man is attracted to you, he won't be forming an opinion based on what you say; he will be picking up primarily on non-verbal clues. So any quick off-the-cuff question will do ('Have you ever read anything by this author?', 'Isn't it crowded in here today?'). Make sure you use questions that will encourage him to continue the conversation. I know you may be thinking that you could never be as forward as this – and maybe you really are too shy to do more than smile. And of course he might ignore you or be married or totally unsuitable, but, hey, as in life so in love: if you won't ever take a risk, nothing new will ever happen. Flirts flirt with life, so get out there and get flirting. Who knows who might be waiting to meet you? If you keep on with the 'same old, same old' routines you will only get the same old result.

Six guerrilla self-marketing techniques

1 Closely examine your routines – where you go, when you go, what you do and who is around you.
2 Organise this information into a series of seven lists, one for each day of the week.

3   Select two things on each day's list that you will change. Specify exactly what you will be doing differently. These are your short-term goals.

4   Choose a few different conversation starters that you can use as icebreakers. Memorise them and be ready to use them at any opportunity.

5   Create some strategic answers that you can use to answer casual questions. Practise so that you feel socially adept and confident.

6   Remember that a natural flirt can always rely on her sexual dynamism and love of life to bring a light-hearted style to the manhunt. If all else fails, you can rely on this.

Getting intimate

Dr Timothy Perper spent over 2,000 hours in singles bars researching the early courting moves made by men and women. He found that when both partners kept to a specific set of moves, they would leave the bar together or make a future date. But if one person (even accidentally) broke the sequence of moves, the couple would drift away from each other. These are the six sub-conscious body language moves that couples must make in order for intimacy to develop. If you are trying to get up close and personal, make sure that you follow them.

Move 1: Make a non-verbal signal. One or the other makes a bodily gesture to show interest (smiling, glancing etc.).

Move 2: Start talking. Verbal communication occurs between the man and woman: a comment, a question or just 'hello'.

Move 3: Show receptivity. After one partner has spoken, the other *must* turn their head to face the speaker and positively acknowledge the comment. If this doesn't happen, the person speaking is very unlikely to try again. If there is a warm response, gradually the two will turn their whole bodies so that they are facing each other completely (head to head, torso-to-torso, knees-to-knees). This sequence can happen immediately or may take some hours, but every time the man and woman move to face each other there will be an increase in intimacy.

Move 4: Start touching. As verbal communication continues and the partners gradually turn to face each other, they will move into the sexually charged touching phase. When she brushes his hand or he touches her arm the next big signal is sent. If the touch does not get a positive response, the toucher will feel rejected and the intimacy will end. But if the first touch is well received, the man and woman will become a couple (if only for the evening).

Move 5: Gaze at each other. After they have touched, the couple change their eye contact from looking to gazing, their eyes beginning to travel over the other's face, hair, neck and body. This escalating eye contact acts as a powerful aphrodisiac.

Move 6: Synchronise movements. Once the couple have established their attraction for each other, they begin an amazing dance of synchronised movements. They may pick up their drinks simultaneously and then put their glasses down at the same time. They start to 'mirror' each other, shifting their weight or swaying to the music together and even copying each other's expressions.

One final point: if there is real magnetism between the two of you, you will automatically make these moves. You will simply be doing what comes naturally when two people are sexually attracted to each other.

Just get flirting

So there you have it. Natural flirts invite attention because they are full of life and buzzing with enthusiasm. But even they sometimes have to follow a strategic plan if they are on the lookout for a partner. I know that some of these tips might seem contrived, but the reality is that *they do work*. So if you are a girl who wants a relationship, you can either wait for someone fabulous to miraculously walk into your life (an unlikely and romantic dream) or you can get out there and take the initiative. As you have seen, you will not frighten a man away if you subtly make the overtures (he will always think that he is in control!). So what have you got to lose? If you make a play for someone and it doesn't work out, you have still demonstrated your great flirting skills, and this will only increase your confidence in the dating arena. If you want a partner, don't sit at home waiting in vain; get out and about and flirt your way to success.

MEDITATION MOMENT

CHARGE YOURSELF WITH POSITIVE ENERGY

Use this simple yoga technique to strengthen your personal electro-magnetic field and revitalise yourself with powerful positive energy.

- Sit comfortably either on the floor or in a chair. Make sure that your back is straight.
- Raise your arms above your head so that they make a V shape (arms about 60 degrees apart).
- Make a half fist with your hands (palms facing forward and thumbs upward).
- Focus your eyes on the point between your eyebrows (you will not be able to see this point, but take your attention in its direction).
- Inhale quickly and strongly through the nose and follow with a longer exhale. Keep your arms straight.
- Carry on inhaling and exhaling in this way for one to two minutes.
- Finally, inhale deeply, hold the breath for a few moments and feel the positive charge of energy coursing through your body and your aura.
- Exhale completely and relax, relax, relax.

Part Two

WINNING THE GAME OF LOVE

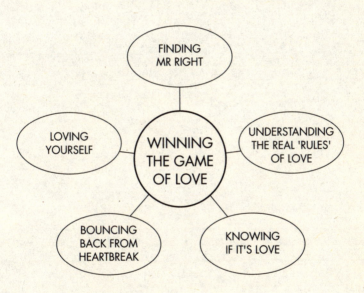

Finding Mr Right

You can look at a guy and really, really want to go to bed with him, but I don't think you can fall in love instantly. You have to get to know the person. Many women want their knights in shining armour to come along and sweep them off their feet, but in reality, Prince Charming could very well ride up on his horse and fall off.

JACKIE COLLINS, AUTHOR OF
23 ROMANTIC NOVELS

Tonight I am rushing: I haven't met my daily word target for this book; I've had interviews with three magazines and done two life coaching sessions; and all day I've been aware that the cupboards are bare and we need a food shop. Then, just moments ago, my husband rang to say he would be a bit late home because he was going to Tesco's. And for what feels like the millionth time in our marriage I feel gratitude and appreciation for an act which to me qualifies as a truly great romantic gesture. Sure, I like roses, Belgian chocolates, champagne, gifts, candlelit dinners etc., but most of all I value the teamwork that goes into our relationship. For me, true romance is to be found in the details of everyday life rather than the odd flamboyant and extravagant gesture.

When I first met Richard he was looking after his son, keeping a house together and writing a book, and these things told me a lot about him. Of course I fancied him like mad (this sexual attraction *must* exist for a relationship to take off) but just as important for me was this demonstration of his life skills. With two small children in tow I needed all the usual things (great sex, adoration etc.), but I also had to have a man who could look after my children and knew how to use the oven. Hence I knew that a Mr Right for me would have to be well qualified in the domestic department.

The first time he invited me round to his place there was a warm apple strudel on a baking tray just out of the oven. My heart was won! Here he was, the man of my dreams: childcare expert, intelligent, thoughtful, sensitive *and* master baker. It wasn't until 15 years later that he told me the cake was from Marks and Spencer. But the point was that he not only wanted to impress me but he actually *knew* how to impress me – and he still does. So the fact that he went to the supermarket tonight was right in character; he is a man who is quite happy to shop and cook, and I still value these remarkable qualities.

If you are looking for a long-term relationship, you must get smart about it. Wallowing around in PEA-induced lust blindness will not necessarily bring you closer to your goal. Yes, sexual chemistry is important but *this alone* does not necessarily mean that he is right for you. Talk to any woman who is in a good, lasting relationship and you will find that she made a careful choice, based on what she knew she wanted from a man.

A man who is right for you (who conforms with your must-have checklist) is not the same as the one and only Mr Right (hero of your romantic dreams). Step out of fantasy and into reality and your chances of striking lucky increase dramatically. You know that saying, 'Don't go food shopping when you are starving'? Well, apply the same logic to your love life. Don't turn your next date into a romantic fantasy figure just because you are desperate for a relationship. Get clear about what sort of man you want. Decide what qualities he needs to possess and shop wisely!

There is all the difference between a man who is right for you and Mr Right. The time we spend looking for The One is always counter-productive. When we buy into the belief that our soulmate is somewhere out there and we only have to find him, we have become victims of love and we will never be satisfied. Mr Perfect does not exist, and even if he did and you met him, can you imagine the pressure you would be under to live up to his faultless talents? Love myths are dangerous because they cloud our judgement and stop us from making good relationship choices and achieving our love goals.

Four dangerous love myths

1 Mr Right is out there somewhere. Have you ever found yourself thinking 'Is he the one?'? This question presupposes that there is one ideal mate for each of us and unless we meet him we cannot be truly happy. But imagine the incredible odds involved in the possibility of us meeting this one person. How would we ever know where to find him? Of course, most of us fall in love more than once, which implies that there are many potential partners out there.

When we are single and looking for *the one*, we may find ourselves judging every love interest to see if he fits the bill. As *the one* is Mr Perfect, we are likely to be forever checking men out against a list of 'perfect' credentials. Surely *the one* would be more handsome? He wouldn't be divorced. He would be earning more money . . . And so we might easily miss out on a great relationship just because a guy has faults. And once we are in a relationship and things get rocky, there may be that underlying sneaky suspicion that maybe he isn't *the one* after all. This can lead us to give up too quickly, not realising that we make a relationship work with our time, effort, commitment and love. Being in love with a fantasy figure leaves us unable to see the real man who stands in front of us.

Mel, 39, is a sales executive whose husband died tragically in a car crash eight years ago. Since then Mel has been on a number of dates, usually set up by friends. She says, 'I've met some interesting men but none that could compare with my darling Sean. I just know that no one will ever fit into his shoes, he was my soulmate.' And of course no one ever will, because every relationship we have is different. If Mel ever wants a new relationship, she will have to let go of her belief that there is only one true love to be had.

The happy reality is that there may be many possible

partners for each of us. Keep an open mind and an open heart and forget about Mr Right. The Mr Right fantasy might mean that you miss out on the chance of creating a wonderful relationship with a real man (who will have his faults!). Compatibility and love are the key requirements for a healthy partnership.

2 As long as I love him enough nothing else matters. Ah, true love always wins the day. We see this message everywhere – in movies, magazines and romantic novels – and *we long to believe it*! I can't tell you how many clients have expressed the belief that if only they can love their man (Mr Right) *enough*, they will be able to make their relationship work. Have you ever thought this? What exactly does it mean to love *enough*, and enough for whom?

Think about your present relationship (if you are in one) and also any past relationship in which you have felt that loving enough was the answer to any problem that might arise between you. Finish the following statement. Do this at least three times for each partner:

As long as I love him enough it won't matter that . . .

These are some of the responses I have received from clients who have done this exercise:

- . . . he often criticises me
- . . . he's always talking about his ex
- . . . he is low in confidence and often very negative

- . . . our sex life doesn't satisfy me
- . . . I don't always trust him
- . . . he looks at other women when I am out with him
- . . . he drinks too much
- . . . he doesn't want children and I do
- . . . I can't really talk to him about how I am feeling
- . . . he often loses his temper
- . . . he's younger than me and keeps throwing it in my face
- . . . I want to move but he doesn't
- . . . I do all the domestic work
- . . . he sometimes makes fun of me in front of other people

We have all succumbed to this myth at some time. I have yet to meet a woman who has never ever thought that loving will make everything better.

Bella, 31, is a journalist. She married Fred, 32, a teacher, three years ago, and they are now separated. When they met, Bella fell head over heels in love. She says, 'Fred treated me like a princess. Nothing was too good for me, and he showered me with presents and adoration. I was sure that he was the love of my life. I felt so special, and all my friends were envious. We got married quickly and it was all like a fabulous dream come true. But soon I realised that the way Fred treated me was more about keeping me under his thumb than anything else. When I had to go away for work, he would get very angry and withdrawn, and I didn't feel like his princess any more. He used all his charming flattery to hide what he really wanted, which was to control me. Whenever I asserted myself, he became aggressive, and sometimes he even hit me. I was sure at the time that our love for each other would heal the rift and make everything better, and I did try to calm him down and reassure him when he lost his temper. I thought that if we had a baby he might feel more settled, but I hadn't conceived after six months, and he got mad about that. In the end he wore out my love for him, and I saw that he was really a control freak who wanted to beat me into submission (literally). I still couldn't bring myself to leave him, and then he pushed me downstairs and I broke my ankle. It was then that I realised it was all over and I left.'

Believing that loving enough *is* enough, allows us to deny our relationship difficulties. Underlying this is the belief that if we love enough we can change a man, and so it is that some women stay in poor relationships, living forever in hope! Relationships cannot live on the idea of love; there has to be *love in action*. This means commitment, compatibility, trust and teamwork; these are the components of a healthy and lasting love relationship.

3 The perfect partner will complete me. This particular belief proves the kiss of death to any love affair. Remember how your relationships reflect the way you feel about yourself. If you are confident and have self-respect, others will treat you well, and if you are low in self-esteem, others will pick this up and mirror your lack of self-worth. No one can make you feel better about yourself; it has to come from you. Your partner can never fulfil the needs you should be fulfilling yourself. Get a life and then get a man is good advice, because it means that you are emotionally independent when you enter a relationship. You know how to stand on your own two feet and you are not making impossible or unreasonable demands of your partner. Self-confidence comes from within and leads to relationship confidence.

If you enter a relationship with an empty space inside, do not expect your partner to fill it. He cannot complete you by supplying the missing pieces in your life, and you will inevitably be disappointed and resentful. Why do we expect another person to get our lives on track when we are the only ones who can do this? My first marriage failed because I wasn't happy with myself, and being married only made this more obvious to me. I had two beautiful children who brought me great joy, but it still wasn't enough. It is a sad irony that becoming a single mother was the making of me (I had no one to blame or to lean on; I just had to get it together).

When you are in a healthy relationship with a partner who is right for you, he will indeed fulfil many of your needs, but he can never satisfy all of them. Recognise the issues that arise because you need to make some personal changes, and then get on and make them. For example, if you feel taken for granted at work, you will come home miserable every day. Only you can alter this situation (by being more assertive or changing your job). Your partner can support you and encourage you, but that is all he can do; he cannot make it right for you. Loving relationships create a supportive framework within which both partners can evolve and grow. The poet Kahlil Gibran expresses this beautifully in his wonderful poem 'The Prophet':

And stand together, yet not too near together:
For the pillars of the temple stand apart,
And the oak tree and the cypress grow not in each
*   other's shadow.*

4 The sex is great; it must be love. A healthy relationship needs good sex, that's for sure, but having good sex does not necessarily mean that you have a healthy relationship. You might be a fantastic match between the sheets but not so good outside of the bed. Men can live with this situation much more easily than women (surprise surprise!). Most of us girls feel guilty enjoying sex for its own sake and imagine that we must have romantic feelings for our object of desire. Let yourself off this hook. If you crave a sexual encounter with a gorgeous man who turns you on, why feel bad about it? No strings attached, casual sex definitely has something going for it, and if this is what you want then recognise your lust for what it is and don't dress it up as love (just make sure you practise safe sex). Perhaps you have fantasised about a man and pursued him – you were sure it must be love – only to discover that it was a purely sexual attraction. It's OK to experience lust when it isn't love, but it's not OK to pretend that the relationship is more than it is. Here lies trouble. Barbara De Angelis explains how we are inclined to legitimise our sexual activity by taking the following steps. She calls this the 'Lust into Love Formula'.

Step 1 You have the hots for someone, you lust after his body, you can't stop thinking about having sex with him.
Step 2 You have sex with him.
Step 3 You feel uncomfortable and maybe guilty that you acted out your fantasies.
Step 4 You create an emotional relationship with your lover to sanction your lust.

If we believe that a good sex life equals a good love life, we are playing with fire. Maria, 28, is PA to the CEO of a large international company. Her boss (we will call him James) is married with three children and is (in her words) 'desperately attractive'. Maria began sleeping with James a few years ago on a trip to Amsterdam and says that she fell 'totally in love'. Maria knows that their liaison is going nowhere further, and although her gorgeous, powerful and unattainable boss is quite happy with the arrangement, she is not. She says, 'The sex is so fantastic, and as we work together there is always a great build-up of tension between us. I know I am addicted to the excitement of being his mistress. He will never leave his wife, and I will never have him for myself, but every other man pales in comparison with him. I am trapped by my sexual desire for him.'

But, of course, we can have sex and love; in fact, we must have both if we want a relationship that will last. Sexual chemistry keeps us going when we hit the turbulent waves in our relationship, and our love for our partner helps us through whenever the flames of passion cool. Let's face it, we bring all of ourselves to our relationship (the good, the bad and the ugly), and so does our partner. However much in love you are, there will be days when he irritates the hell out of you and you drive him crazy, but that's life! You are not perfect and neither is he; he may not be your fantasy Mr Right, but if you have chosen well, he will be right for you.

What do you look for in a man?

Socialite Paris Hilton says, 'Sexy, funny and filthy rich: [these are] the three things I look for in a man.' Ah, Paris, if only it was as straightforward as this! Our tastes in men are much more complex than we think, and are linked right back to our early childhood patterning. Whether you find him enchanting or repulsive, sexy or boring, will depend on many unconscious subtleties and nuances.

Dr Stephen Whitehead is an expert on gender who has created a psychological breakdown of 27 types of male. He says that his research will help women to 'be able to tell the bad apples from the good, to spot the stronger men among the weaker ones, to separate the serial seducers from the marrying types'. Journalist Sam Greenhill picked up on this research and ran a piece in the *Daily Mail* that suggested a celebrity to go with each profile. For example, Alastair Campbell personified the Alpha Male (ruthless in pursuit of his goals), Del Boy was the Risker (pushes his luck too far), Robbie Williams was a Zebedee (confused

INSTANT TIP

GET REAL ABOUT YOU

IT TAKES TWO TO TANGO, SO LET'S TAKE A REALISTIC LOOK AT WHAT YOU BRING TO YOUR RELATIONSHIP. IF YOU ARE NOT WITH A PARTNER AT THE MOMENT, THINK ABOUT HOW YOU THOUGHT, FELT AND BEHAVED IN A PREVIOUS RELATIONSHIP. COMPLETE THE FOLLOWING STATEMENTS.

- I SHOW MY LOVE BY . . . .
- I AM DISAPPOINTED WHEN HE . . . .
- I CAN'T FORGIVE HIM WHEN . . . .
- MY WORST CHARACTERISTIC IS . . . .
- I TEND TO FEEL CLINGY WHEN . . . .
- IF ONLY HE WOULD . . . .
- I FEEL SECURE IN A RELATIONSHIP WHEN . . . .
  . . . .
- I FEEL INSECURE IN A RELATIONSHIP WHEN . . . . .
  . . . .
- WHEN I FEEL CONFIDENT, OUR RELATIONSHIP LOOKS
  . . . .
- WHEN I FEEL LOW IN CONFIDENCE, OUR RELATION-SHIP LOOKS . . . .
- I KNOW I AM A GOOD JUDGE OF CHARACTER, BECAUSE . . . .
- ONE OF THE MISTAKES I HAVE MADE IS . . . .

- I EXPECT HIM TO . . . .
- WHEN HE DOESN'T FULFIL MY EXPECTATIONS I . . .
  . . . .
- OUR SEX LIFE IS . . . .
- I FEEL SEXY WHEN . . . .
- LOVE IS . . . .
- OUR BEST MOMENTS ARE . . . .
- OUR WORST MOMENTS ARE . . . .
- I CAN FORGIVE . . . .
- I THINK THAT WE ARE . . . .
- LONG-TERM RELATIONSHIPS FEEL . . . .
- I WISH I COULD . . . .
- THE MOST POSITIVE THING ABOUT US IS . . . .
  . . . .
- I AM ATTRACTED TO HIM BECAUSE . . . .

REVIEW YOUR ANSWERS AND GET REAL ABOUT WHO
YOU REALLY ARE.

and needy, needs nurturing), Russell Crowe was the
Neanderthal (old-fashioned, with bigoted views on
women), Simon Cowell was Mr Angry (for obvious
reasons) - and so the list goes on. It's quite an amusing
theory, and maybe you can look into your own relationship
history and see if you have a penchant for one of these
particular styles - because there is no doubt that you will
be attracted to certain sorts of men and repelled by others.

So why, for example, might we go for tall blond guys with blue eyes who are good at sport, while our best friend is attracted to intellectual Celtic types? And how come we can keep attracting the same 'brand' of man even when we know he is bad news for us?

Discover your Lovemap

We manufacture the love drug PEA in response to certain stimuli that turn us on at the deepest level. When we are very young, we subconsciously absorb and retain any experiences of pain and pleasure that make a powerful impression on us; this process is called sexual imprinting. Sexologists use the concept of Lovemaps to describe how this works. Each of us has a Lovemap that includes both the positive and the negative imprinting which causes us to be sexually attracted to other people. This explains why we feel excited and also helpless in the very first stages of falling in love. You know what this is like – it's almost as if you have lost all control and have no choice but to go the way of your heart.

Think of the times when you have been moved to emotional madness by a superficial assessment of a man – perhaps because you were smitten by his eyes or his hair. It has been said that we take more care and spend more time buying a new handbag than we do evaluating a new love interest. We are totally at the mercy of our sexual imprinting until we get to know the contents of our personal Lovemaps.

When my client Kate first met the dark, brooding and

introverted Dominic, she turned into a quivering jelly and couldn't stop talking about him for days. Eventually she asked him out on a date. By this time she was in a state of frenzy. Next morning I rang to see how it had gone. Kate was as flat as a pancake. She said that he had been an utter bore all evening and seemed unable to put more than a few simple words together. His vocabulary was not very large and he really had nothing to say. So much for the elusive hidden depths that had so captivated her.

If a certain smile or look or swagger of the hips can turn you weak at the knees, then recognise this. Get off on the buzz but don't expect it to lead you up the aisle. 'Helpless' and 'hopeless' are words often used to describe the way we feel when we are high on the love drug, but you and I both know that these are not the words you want to describe you. By all means love the romance and the first buzz of attraction, but recognise that you must go beyond your sexual imprinting if you are ever going to have a loving and lasting relationship. A man who is right for you will need a lot more than a cute lop-sided grin for things to develop beyond the first few days.

E X E R C I S E :

Check out your Lovemap*

1 Do you favour certain physical features in a man? If so, what specifically do you usually fall for?

2 How would you describe the type of man that most attracts you?

3 Which positive qualities do your past lovers share?

4 Which negative qualities do your past lovers share (look back at your answers to 'Your Love Choices' on page 41).

5 Would you say that you always go for the same type, or for a range of types?

6 Do these types really suit you?

7 Do relationships with your favourite type often end in tears?

8 What conclusions do you draw from your answers?

* Adapted from my book, *Weekend Life Coach*

Attracting Mr Totally Wrong

It will be easy to recognise your positive imprintings. If your darling grandfather loved cricket and football, you might find yourself attracted to sporty men. Or if your father was a motorbike enthusiast, you might have a soft spot for any man who rides up on a Harley Davidson. Check your preferred physical characteristics with the men in your immediate family. Does your latest love interest bear any resemblance to your brother or your male cousins? Do these blond, blue-eyed surfing types you always fancy look like your own father in his heyday? These imprintings are fun to detect and are quite harmless in themselves, unless of course they are the only thing that is holding your relationship together.

INSTANT TIP

YOUR MUST-HAVE CHECKLIST

IT'S TIME TO START THINKING ABOUT THE POSITIVE ATTRIBUTES THAT YOU WANT FROM A MAN. YOU DON'T NEED TO GET TOO SPECIFIC AT THIS STAGE; JUST WRITE DOWN THE FIRST TEN THINGS THAT COME TO MIND.

HE MUST HAVE/MUST BE:

1 . . . . . .
2 . . . . . .
3 . . . . . .
4 . . . . . .
5 . . . . . .
6 . . . . . .
7 . . . . . .
8 . . . . . .
9 . . . . . .
10 . . . . . .

NOW TAKE THE THREE MOST IMPORTANT MUST-HAVES.

DOES YOUR PRESENT PARTNER HAVE THESE QUALITIES?

IF YOU ARE NOT IN A RELATIONSHIP, LOOK BACK AT THE PAST. DID YOUR LAST PARTNER HAVE THEM?

OR THE ONE BEFORE?

REFLECT ON YOUR REPLIES AND THINK THROUGH THEIR IMPLICATIONS.

It is the negative aspects of our Lovemaps that cause the problems. This helps to explain why we sometimes make very poor relationship choices. Following our sexual imprinting, we may find ourselves falling for Mr Totally Wrong over and over again. If this sounds like you, take heart. The first step in changing our behaviour patterns is to recognise what we keep repeating and why. Awareness is your key to self-change. So if you have a poor relationship history and keep falling for men who are inappropriate, cheer up; you can change this behaviour. In fact, you must if you are looking for a loving and nurturing relationship.

If you are having a relationship with an emotionally distant man, you are not alone. Many female clients tell me that their partners are cold and withdrawn and then go on to reveal that their own father was unable to show his feelings. If as a tiny girl you had to beg and plead for attention and love from your father (who you idolised), it's easy to see how it might become your adult life's work to get a man to show his affection for you. You can begin to break this pattern by not having relationships with men who are aloof and remote. Apply this method to any repeated imprintings in your Lovemap that don't work for you. If you are caught in any negative attraction traps do the following:

- Recognise the negative behaviour that is attracting you.
- Decide that you deserve to avoid emotional pain.
- Go for an entirely different type (even though this might be quite difficult at first).

- Remember that you attract whoever you think you deserve.

And of course you deserve the best! You can choose who you love. Stop being a victim of love and forget all about the divine but impossible, one and only Mr Right. Don't limit yourself in this way. Oh, and also forget about Mr Totally Wrong, unless you think that you deserve to be treated badly. Look out for positive and upbeat men (yes, they do exist) and step out with a confident tread. Love magnets know their own worth and are only interested in men who also recognise their talents. It doesn't take long to discover whether a man has it in him to value you. Ask yourself the following questions:

- How does he talk?
- Is he positive about himself and about you?
- How does he treat others?
- Does he support you and cheer you on?
- Is he close to his own family?
- Does he have your best interests at heart?
- How many must-haves does he score on your checklist?

Take off your blindfold, rose-coloured spectacles and anything else that obscures your true vision. Get real about what you want and what you don't want in a man and then get looking for one who is *right for you*!

Love is in the air

And for those of you who think I have lost all sense of romance and excitement in pursuit of positive love goals, here is a story to touch your hearts and remind you that Mr Right for You might arrive on a bus, on a milk-white charger, on a Harley Davidson – or even from the air!

As his warplane plummeted towards the village below, Flight Commander Ted Cowling had only the calm voice of the WAAF operator in the control tower to help him land safely. When his plane touched the ground, Ted was determined to find the woman who had saved his life. Their fateful meeting led to a marriage of 57 years.

This Valentine's Day, Ted and Joy Cowling were named romantic couple of the year at the Asda/NSPCC Valentine's Day award ceremony in a London hotel. Mr Cowling (83) said: 'She had a lovely voice, and when I landed, I knew I owed my life to her. I went up to the control tower and I knocked on the hatch door. When I saw her, I was smitten. She was beautiful – she still is. I certainly thought she was a bit of all right. I made a dinner date with her, and we didn't look back.'

Mrs Cowling (78) shared her secret for a long and happy marriage: 'You have to respect and care for each other. We have been through some bad times, but we carried on working on our marriage and have never given up. We lean on each other when we need to, and Ted is always very loving and romantic and gives me a rose every Valentine's Day.' She added, 'We are in love; we've never fallen out of love. We still hold hands, even if it's just to help each other stand up!' What a great story.

One of the other couples that reached the finals had met when they crashed into each other in a car park. It just goes to show that true romance might be round any corner you take. So keep that romantic flag flying and go for your positive love goals.

MEDITATION MOMENT

WHAT DO YOU SEE IN YOUR MAN?

HAVE YOU A MAN IN YOUR LIFE AT THE MOMENT? THIS COULD BE SOMEONE YOU ARE LIVING WITH, HAVING AN AFFAIR WITH, SHARING CHILDREN WITH OR JUST SOMEONE YOU THINK ABOUT A LOT (IF YOU THINK ABOUT HIM FREQUENTLY, HE IS DEFINITELY IN YOUR LIFE!) IF NO ONE COMES TO MIND, CHOOSE A PERSON FROM A PAST RELATIONSHIP.

SIT COMFORTABLY AND UNWIND. SLOW YOUR BREATHING DOWN AND FEEL YOUR BODY BECOMING MORE AND MORE RELAXED. AS YOUR THOUGHTS DRIFT AWAY, VISUALISE AN EMPTY SCREEN IN YOUR MIND.

WHEN YOU ARE READY, SEE YOUR MAN ON THE SCREEN. SEE HIM IN GLORIOUS TECHNICOLOR. OBSERVE HIM AND BECOME AWARE OF THE THOUGHTS THAT YOU CONNECT WITH HIM, FOR EXAMPLE: *HE'S GETTING FAT; HE IS JUST LIKE HIS DAD; HE'S ABSOLUTELY GORGEOUS;*

HE'S GOT NO SENSE OF STYLE; WHY DOESN'T HE GET HIMSELF TOGETHER?; WHY IS HE ALWAYS SO CRITICAL?; HE IS SUCH A KIND MAN; HE TREATS ME WELL; WHY CAN'T I TRUST HIM?; WHY DOESN'T HE SPEND MORE TIME WITH THE CHILDREN?; HE IS SO GENEROUS; IS HE HAVING AN AFFAIR?; I AM LUCKY TO HAVE HIM.

YOUR internal dialogue will reveal a lot about your feelings for this man. Sometimes we are so busy just living that we forget to stand back and get a real feel for what is going on. This technique gives us the space to be a bit more objective than we usually are. What did you learn from this visualisation?

Understanding the Real 'Rules' of Love

Frankly, many women we know find it easier to relocate to another state, switch careers, or run a marathon than get the right man to marry them! If this sounds like you, then you need The Rules! What are The Rules? They are a simple way of acting around men that can help any woman win the heart of the man of her dreams.

ELLEN FEIN AND SHERRIE SCHNEIDER,
AUTHORS OF *THE RULES*

The following are just a few choice pieces of advice from May 1955's *Housekeeping Monthly* magazine. (You can find the whole article on the Internet; just type 'good wife' into a search engine.)

- Have dinner ready. Plan ahead, even the night before, to have a delicious meal ready, on time for his return. This is a way of letting him know that you have been thinking about him and are concerned about his needs.

- Prepare yourself. Take 15 minutes to rest so that you'll be refreshed when he arrives. Touch up your make-up, put a ribbon in your hair and be fresh-looking. He has just been with a lot of work-weary people.
- Minimise all noise. At the time of his arrival, eliminate all the noise of the washer, dryer or vacuum. Try to encourage the children to be quiet.
- Greet him with a warm smile and show sincerity in your desire to please him.
- Don't ask him questions about his actions or question his judgement or integrity. Remember he is the master of the house and as such will always exercise his will with fairness and truthfulness. You have no right to question him.
- A good wife always knows her place.

I know, you're not sure whether to be scandalised or to laugh your socks off. Perhaps the most common reaction is, 'We've come a long way, girls', but when I read the book *The Rules*, by Ellen Fein and Sherrie Schneider, I wondered just how far we had really come. This million-copy bestseller dedicates itself to teaching women how to play hard to get and how to let the man think he is taking the lead in all things. The authors advise us not to get sloppy about our looks and to keep fit if we want our man to 'keep drooling' over us; to end the relationship if we don't get jewellery or some other romantic gift on our birthday; to be mysterious and act in a ladylike way; not to say much and let him do all the talking; to have interesting novels or non-fiction books lying around our flat so he gets a good impression (and to hide any self-help books!); to always show 'utter contentment' with him because he will desire us more; and (just wait for this), to read newspapers so that we can talk to him about something other than our work or dirty nappies because apparently men 'want wives who can fulfil them mentally as well as physically and emotionally'.

This view hardly fits with our concept of the confident and assertive love magnet and sex goddess; indeed, it sounds suspiciously like *Housekeeping Monthly*'s advice to me. These old 1950s rules are based on the principle that women are lost without a man and that snagging a husband (any husband, it would seem) is our top priority.

Another unspoken rule is that all single people are out there socialising and having a great time. When you are on your own, however, life sometimes seems to revolve around twosomes. Even if you love the freedom of the single lifestyle, you may still experience moments when life in the fast lane feels a bit flat and you start to panic about your unpartnered status. And if your biological clock is ticking and/or all your friends are pairing off, you might easily find yourself having the odd Bridget Jones moment. I remember walking in a park in Bristol, pushing my children in a double buggy. Everywhere I looked there were couples, and I felt such a failure. To a newly separated woman it seemed as if the entire world was happily married. Of course, this was far from the truth. I soon discovered that there were definite advantages to being single (especially after being in a bad relationship).

Whenever you feel alarmed by your single status, just remember these two important things. First, the grass is definitely not always greener in the paradise of marriage, so enjoy being footloose and fancy free while you can. Second, you are more likely to meet a great guy if you just slack off a bit and stop trying so hard. Forget any advice that suggests you put on some sort of act in order to date and 'catch' a man. These old rules are based on such desperate thoughts as:

- I am incomplete without a man.
- I need a man to fall in love with me.
- I want to be just what he wants me to be.
- I must get him to marry me.

Any action you take while in this state of mind will not work to your advantage. When you find yourself musing over such words as 'spinster' or 'left on the shelf', stop immediately and take a reality check. Remember that you are a fascinating and interesting woman who is independent and assertive. Because you respect yourself and have a life of your own, you are a strong and attractive love magnet. As a woman of taste and discernment, you are never prepared to settle for less than the best in life, and this includes your love life.

Suzanne is 54 and runs a smallholding with her son. She is a child of the fifties, and her parents had old-fashioned views about men and women and the roles they should play. Suzanne's mother always told her that she needed only to marry a man who was a 'good provider' and then she would be settled for life. Some of Suzanne's contemporaries stayed on at grammar school and went to university, but Suzanne's parents encouraged her to leave school at 16 and take secretarial training. Suzanne says, 'I never considered having a serious career, as I had been brought up with the expectation that I would marry, settle down and look after my husband and my family, which, of course, is exactly what my mother did. And that might have been all right if I had had the confidence to know my own mind and to make a good relationship choice. When I was 19 I met Philip, who was an apprentice in the local garage, and he asked me on a date. He was the first man who had ever asked me out, and my parents and I were so relieved that I was 'normal' and 'courting'. And so I was just swept into it. Honestly, I never even considered that there were other men out there; I was just glad to be 'chosen', and I was so proud when we got engaged. Looking back at it all, it seems so crazy. After a three-year engagement we got married and I quickly became pregnant. I had four children with a boring and insensitive man who was only really interested in car engines, football and drinking with his mates. I stuck it out until our youngest child left home and then I moved away and retrained at the local agricultural college. Philip couldn't believe it when I left him, and he never knew that I had been waiting to get away from him for 30 years. If I had only known then what I know now, I would have stood up for myself and created a different life. Because getting married was my goal, I never realised that it mattered *who* I married and I never had the confidence to be assertive with my husband. I enjoy my single life now and I run my own business and make my own decisions. Well, I got there in the end.'

When desperation can get you into trouble

The old rules will keep you in chains, because they are based on negative and fearful thoughts that go something like this. *I am afraid: of being alone, of being unattractive to a man, of saying too much and giving myself away, of him getting tired of me, of not being the right woman for him, of not being good enough . . .* and the rest! Look at the following diagram, which shows what can happen when we come from this fear-based place of low self-worth.

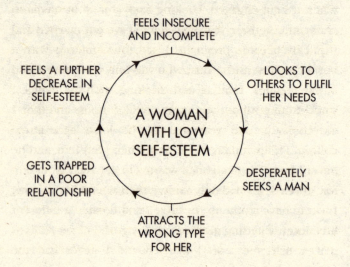

FEELS INSECURE AND INCOMPLETE

LOOKS TO OTHERS TO FULFIL HER NEEDS

A WOMAN WITH LOW SELF-ESTEEM

DESPERATELY SEEKS A MAN

ATTRACTS THE WRONG TYPE FOR HER

GETS TRAPPED IN A POOR RELATIONSHIP

FEELS A FURTHER DECREASE IN SELF-ESTEEM

When we are low in self-esteem we feel incomplete and are inclined to look for someone else to fill the empty places inside us. Single women who have little self-esteem are often desperate to have a relationship with a man in order that they can feel worthwhile. Men pick up on this neediness, and it frightens many of them away. Because such women are acting like victims, they often attract the sort of man who likes to bully women (victims are a magnet for bullies). At the least they attract the wrong type of man and then find themselves trapped in a poor relationship. And so their self-esteem takes yet another knock, and they feel even emptier than when they were on their own.

Money can't buy it!

Actress Jerry Hall confesses: 'I feel empty. I act because it fills the time. It feeds me. You know what the greatest challenge is? Love. It is love that I have never managed, that I have yet to conquer.' Jerry is a woman who was desperate for Mick's attention and who forfeited her happiness for their relationship. Although she was drastically unhappy, she stayed with him for 25 years in the hope that he would change his ways. Here is an example of a woman who appears to have everything and yet she struggles with self-esteem. She felt 'empty' and so she looked to Mick to make her feel complete – big mistake! So if brains, beauty, wealth and fame can't guarantee self-esteem, what can?

Low self-esteem drags us into poor relationships with

men who are stuck in the old rules. They like to be in control and don't like confident women. They believe that 'boys will be boys'. They are determined to do their own thing (whatever this is) regardless of how it affects their partner. They expect a woman to know her place (which is beneath them!). If you have been in a relationship with a man like this and have managed to leave, you have done so by working on your self-esteem.

Denise, 33, is a full-time mother of two who spent six years in a marriage with a man who chased other women. After the first affair she was devastated, but she and her husband both had counselling and things seemed to settle down again. Then, while she was pregnant with their second child, Denise discovered an earring in the back of the car. Her husband told her that the woman who owned it had meant nothing to him and was just a one-night fling. She said, 'I stayed because I felt that I had to make it work and I was feeling so vulnerable as I was only three weeks away from giving birth. I forgave him, and he was so loving and tender for the next few months that I began to feel guilty for causing such a fuss (I can't believe this now!). He really was like a changed man, but there was a hidden part of me that couldn't quite trust him any more (and I felt guilty about this too!). About a year after our second child was born, I began to feel uneasy, as my husband had started to work away one night a week, but I pretended to myself that we were OK. Then, one night when he was away, my best friend came round with a bottle of wine, and I broke down and told her what I thought was going on. I had never told her about the times before because I felt too ashamed. I cried for hours, and it was so good just to let it all out. The next night I confronted my husband. He just collapsed and said that his latest conquest was not important to him and it was 'only a casual affair' (as if that made it all right). This was the last straw. I felt humiliated and very angry. I suddenly saw for the first time how I had let him treat me and I knew I couldn't put up with it a moment longer. We divorced, and I still see him when he sees the kids. But I look at him now and can't believe that I put up with him. He seems so weak. I was so low in self-esteem that I felt trapped in that marriage, and it wasn't until I really snapped that I found the strength in me to regain control of my life. I have really grown since the divorce and I am twice the woman I was when we got married. I would like to have a relationship again one day, but it would have to be an equal and supportive one. Meanwhile I go out with men occasionally, and I am working on an Open University degree course.'

Learning to say no

Learning to say no is one of the most important issues for anyone with low self-esteem. It means verbally saying no when you don't want to do something, and also means putting your foot down when necessary. What might have happened to Jerry and Mick if she had stood up for herself all those years ago? Have you ever been in a relationship where you could have said no and didn't? What were the consequences?

EXERCISE:

What stops you saying no?

The purpose of this exercise is to become aware of your underlying reasons for not being able to say no. Think about any time when you wished you had said no but didn't. This might have been with a partner or with anyone else. Imagine yourself right there in the situation again, and then finish this sentence:

Saying no is hard for me because . . . .

Some of the following reasons are common:

- I feel guilty.
- I want to be liked.
- I'm afraid to make people angry; I never want to rock the boat.
- I don't want to be alone.
- I need this relationship to work.
- I will do all I can to keep him.
- I'm so attracted to him I just can't say no, even though I know I should.
- I hate hurting people.
- I don't like conflict.
- It's easier to say I will do something and then just not do it.
- I'm a coward when it comes to confrontations.
- It's easier just to say yes.
- I am too frightened to speak up for myself; I'd rather let sleeping dogs lie.

Think carefully about this incident. How did you feel about yourself when you didn't say no? Would you act the same way again?

_____

Whoever you choose to live with, or not to live with, one thing is for sure: you have to live with yourself – and this particular relationship will last forever. Be the person you are glad to live with. Make decisions that support whatever it is that you really want. Be your own best friend and admire and respect yourself. Expect others to treat you well, and stay away from anyone who tries to diminish or demean you in any way. This is your chance, this one life, so value it and hold yourself in high esteem.

INSTANT TIP

REMEMBER THAT HE IS LUCKY TO GET YOU

THE NEXT TIME YOUR NEED TO BE IN A RELATIONSHIP STARTS TO CLOUD YOUR JUDGEMENT ABOUT A MAN, TRY THIS SIMPLE TRICK. WRITE:

HE IS LUCKY TO GET ME BECAUSE:

1 . . . .

2 . . . .

3 . . . .

---

4 . . . .

5 . . . .

6 . . . .

7 . . . .

8 . . . .

9 . . . .

10 . . . .

MAKE SURE YOU FIND TEN REASONS WHY HE IS/WOULD BE VERY FORTUNATE TO GET YOU. INSTEAD OF IMAGINING HIM AS A GREAT 'CATCH', TURN IT AROUND AND SEE WHY *YOU* ARE SUCH AN ATTRACTIVE PROPOSITION. BECOME AWARE OF ALL THE STRENGTHS AND ABILITIES THAT YOU BRING TO THE RELATIONSHIP. REFLECT ON YOUR ADMIRABLE QUALITIES AND YOUR SENSITIVITY. WHAT IS YOUR UNIQUE CONTRIBUTION TO YOUR PARTNERSHIP? SPEND SOME TIME PONDERING THESE POINTS.

YOU SEE, IT'S TRUE; HE IS, OR WOULD BE, VERY LUCKY TO HAVE A RELATIONSHIP WITH YOU.

The real rules for finding the right relationship

These are guidelines that are grounded in a calm and relaxed approach to the mating game. We have seen that low self-esteem can only lead to relationship trouble and so we must draw on our feelings of self-respect and self-worth if we are to get the right man for us. The real relationship rules are based on such positive and assertive beliefs as:

- I am a strong and confident single woman.
- I want a man who is right for me.
- I want him to love the real me.
- I would like our relationship to develop into a lasting commitment.

When you come from a place of high self-esteem, you are always free to be yourself (the real you) in any relationship.

Ten ways to be yourself in a relationship

1 Be true to yourself and don't pretend to be something you are not.
2 Don't try to please a man at your own expense.
3 Never compare yourself with other women; you are good enough just the way you are.
4 Express your real feelings instead of keeping them to yourself.
5 Have high expectations of your relationship; don't settle for less than the best.
6 Refuse to play games to catch and keep a man.
7 Know how far you are prepared to go and say no when you have to.
8 Be honest about what you want and treat men the way you want them to treat you.

9 Stop having a relationship with any man who treats you badly.

10 Don't get involved with a man who is stuck in the old rules.

The Theory of Relationships as Mirrors

Shakti Gawain describes the Theory of Relationships as Mirrors succinctly when she says, 'My true relationship is my relationship with myself – all others are simply mirrors of it.' According to this theory, the type of relationship you attract depends exactly upon the quality of your own thoughts, beliefs and expectations. In other words, the ways in which people react towards you are an exact reflection of how you feel about yourself. It works like this:

THE WAY YOU FEEL ABOUT YOURSELF	THE WAY OTHERS REACT TOWARDS YOU *
High in self-esteem	Respectfully
Angry	With hostility
Judgemental	Critically
Low in self-belief	With lack of trust
Positive	Responsive and receptive
Content and at peace	Harmoniously
Negative	With boredom and a lack of sympathy
Guilty	With blame
Loving	With kindness and caring
Body confident and attractive	With interest, drawn towards you

If you respect yourself, others will pick up on your feelings and treat you well, and if you love and value yourself, you will be loved and valued by others. If you think badly of yourself and are self-critical, others will reflect those feelings back to you. If you regard yourself as a victim, you will attract bullies (victims need bullies, and bullies need victims). If you are low in confidence, you will soon convince everyone that you are no good, useless, pathetic and so on.

When you understand the way that your relationships act as mirrors for your inner self, you can start to change the way you think and behave and so change the type of relationships that you are attracting. If the men in your life are not treating you with respect, check your own levels of self-esteem. Are you putting out a desperate vibe and attracting men who will victimise you? Could you increase your own levels of positivity and make people more responsive and receptive towards you?

Instead of looking outside ourselves and blaming others for our disappointing love lives (this will never provide solutions), we can stop and answer these two questions:

1 What is this relationship showing me about myself?
2 How can I use this insight to improve the quality of the relationships I attract?

Always remember that:

- Our inner selves (thoughts, beliefs, emotions, expectations . . .) create the nature of all of our relationships.

- These relationships can reveal to us new ways of looking at ourselves.
- This knowledge shows us how to create new, improved relationships.

Use this perceptive theory to show you where and how you need to change so that you can become a love magnet.

* Adapted from my book *Weekend Life Coach*

Jeanette, 25, works in advertising. Although she holds down a powerful job, she is much less assertive in the love department. This is how she describes her love life: 'It's a total mess. I can't seem to make any clear decisions about men and I always end up with guys who make me feel worse than useless. Each time, I go for the powerful, ambitious types, then as soon as we get together I start to feel bad about myself. I do all that I can to make it work, and I think I bend over backwards to make things easy for boyfriends, but I always end up feeling unappreciated whatever I do. I am such a supportive person; why do men always treat me badly? I think all men are selfish bores and they are only interested in their own wants and needs.'

So why does Jeanette keep having such lousy relationships? Is it because all men are self-interested? Of course not, this is just a belief she holds which she keeps reinforcing by going for men who will treat her badly. Jeanette admits that she is a poor decision-maker when it comes to men; she repeats the same old behaviour patterns by looking for the same type of man. These patterns (thoughts, feelings, behaviours) are attracting men whose own patterns are victimising and uncaring. Jeanette realised that she would only ever meet a good man if she changed her own behaviour. Using the Theory of Relationships as Mirrors, she was able to recognise that at some level she believed that she deserved to be taken for granted; if she didn't, she would never have allowed any man to treat her like this. She saw that she would carry on having poor relationships until she began to value and respect her own needs.

Once we understand how the reflecting process works, we have an amazing self-development tool at our fingertips. If you want to know where you are at, just look at the people you are in relationships with (lovers, colleagues, friends, family). The quality of your relationships with others reflects the quality of your relationship with yourself. Your relationships begin and end with you; you are in control. You choose the people you attract and whether they will be positive and supportive or blaming and critical. You can choose to use the reflecting process within your relationships to help you to change and move on or you can allow yourself to keep repeating negative patterns by blaming others. If your love life needs an overhaul and you want a fabulous intimate partnership with a man who is there for you, there is only one way to go: *reflect, change and move on!*

INSTANT TIP

CLEAR THE PATH TO YOUR FUTURE

ONCE WE START TO TAKE CONTROL OF OUR LIVES, WE STOP BLAMING OTHERS – BUT THEN SOMETIMES FALL INTO A TRAP OF BLAMING OURSELVES INSTEAD. AS SOON AS WE BEGIN TO CRITICISE OURSELVES, WE HAVE LOST OUR POWER AGAIN AND OUR SELF-ESTEEM DISAPPEARS.

IF YOU ARE LOOKING AT YOUR RELATIONSHIP HISTORY AND RECOGNISING THE PART YOU PLAYED IN ATTRACTING YOUR PARTNERS, YOU CAN USE THIS INFORMATION TO YOUR ADVANTAGE AS LONG AS YOU CAN FORGIVE YOURSELF. THIS MEANS A WHOLE NEW TAKE ON THE WAY YOU VIEW THE 'MISTAKES' YOU THINK YOU MADE. THE PAST IS DONE AND THERE IS NO GOING BACK.

- REALISE THAT WE ALL MAKE MISTAKES; THIS IS THE WAY WE LEARN AND GROW.
- RECOGNISE WHERE YOU WENT WRONG AND THEN DECIDE NOT TO REPEAT THIS AGAIN!
- FORGIVE YOURSELF FOR ALL THE THINGS YOU THINK YOU 'SHOULD' OR 'OUGHT TO' HAVE DONE.
- LET GO OF ALL THE OLD EMOTIONAL CLUTTER THAT FILLS YOUR LIFE AND STOPS YOU MOVING FORWARD.
- LET GO OF YOUR PAST LOVERS (WHATEVER THEY WERE LIKE).
- CLEAR THE PATH THAT LEADS TO YOUR FUTURE AND FREE YOURSELF TO MEET THE RIGHT MAN FOR YOU.

EXERCISE:

Are you a woman with self-esteem?

Read the following statements. Ask yourself if they are true for you.

Score as follows:

1 almost always
2 often
3 sometimes
4 almost never

1 I compare myself unfavourably with other women.

2 When I am single I feel unsettled and on the lookout for a man.

3 The men I attract are not good for me.

4 I find it hard to leave a poor relationship.

5 It is difficult for me to say no.

6 I don't know when or how to put my foot down in a relationship.

7 I am scared that I might never get married.
   Or
   I feel trapped in an unhappy marriage.

8 I want children, so I feel in a rush to meet the right man.
   Or
   I have children and this adversely affects my relationship decisions.

9 Men intimidate me.

10 I wish I could change the past.

If you scored 10–19

Stop a moment and hold it right there! Although you are struggling with your love issues, you have a sliver of hope for yourself because you bought this book. You know that it is possible to change and you even know some ways to start. So begin! Work on yourself, focus on your own needs and start to appreciate the wonderful woman that you are. Take one small step towards a goal right now and start to take control of your life. You can do this. Hundreds of thousands of women have been here before and managed to move on, and so can you. I know you can believe in yourself, even if it feels impossible to you right now. Keep reading this book and doing the exercises; you *will* become a woman with self-esteem.

If you scored 20–29

You have been doing some work on yourself, and it is beginning to show. If you are in a relationship, you are starting to notice how the way you feel about yourself affects the way that your partner treats you. Decide to step right out of that cycle where low self-esteem makes you needy and submissive. You can stand up for yourself; you do know what you really want and you are brave enough to go for it. Stop acting like a mouse and become the woman you would most love to be. You are the only one who can give yourself high self-esteem. Start now!

And if you are single, why not be positive about it? Become an irrepressible life force and step into the power of the singleton, who is free to come and go as she pleases. When you love living by yourself, you are more likely to attract a man who would love to live with you.

If you scored 30–40

You are a woman with self-esteem. Sure, there are moments when you lose it (as we all do at times), but you know how to pick up the pieces and get back on track again. If you are in a relationship, you are aware of what occurs between the two of you and why. Keep using the reflecting process so that you can become clear about how and what you are creating within your intimate relationships.

And if you are single, you are probably enjoying the perks of freedom rather than dwelling on what you might be missing. Keep working on yourself and you will find that you will attract men who are also high in self-esteem. Two people who respect themselves can come together to create a brilliant and nurturing relationship with each other.

A woman with self-esteem knows the real rules of love

Drew Barrymore says: 'I don't buy into the Cinderella theory where you sit around and wait for your perfect prince to rescue you. I want to know that you're going to figure yourself out and on the way find room for the love in your life.' Nicely put, Drew! Stop imagining a fairytale ending and start to 'figure yourself out' – this is the only way forward. A woman with self-esteem is self-contained and self-aware. She knows how to be herself and never compromises her beliefs and behaviour. When you walk into a roomful of people, she is the one who attracts your attention with her inner confidence and self-belief. These qualities make her shine. She only ever uses the real rules of love and so she is happy with her single state until she finds a man who is right for her. Because she isn't looking to be 'rescued' by a man, she has an air of self-knowing-ness and independence that turns her into a man-magnet. But, of course, she never attracts weak or bullying men because they are terrified of her.

This woman is you! As soon as you stop looking to others to make you happy, you will find that you have inner strength and power that you didn't know existed. When you feel insecure (as we all do sometimes), look inside yourself for the answers you seek. No one can give you self-belief and self-esteem; you have to find it inside yourself. As you grow in confidence, you will notice that you draw different types of men into your life. A self-confident woman attracts men who are confident enough to appreciate her. Look at the diagram below and decide

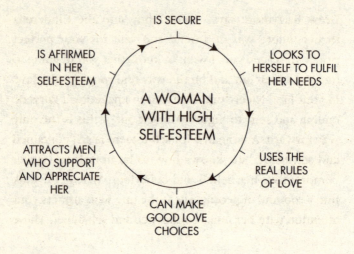

to step into this new cycle. Start now. Believe in yourself and become a woman with high self-esteem who can make good love choices.

MEDITATION MOMENT

THE UNIVERSE SUPPORTS YOU TODAY

RELAX AND UNWIND. PUT YOUR FEET UP AND IMAGINE THAT ALL YOUR WORRIES AND PROBLEMS ARE BEING TAKEN CARE OF. JUST FOR TODAY, ALLOW YOURSELF TO LET UP A LITTLE ON THE DEMAND TO KEEP *ABSOLUTELY EVERYTHING* TOGETHER. TODAY, THE REST OF THE UNIVERSE CAN MANAGE WITHOUT YOU CARRYING ALL THOSE BURDENS.

- DROP YOUR SHOULDERS AND FEEL THE TENSION LIFT.
- WHENEVER YOU FEEL ANXIOUS TODAY, JUST SAY TO YOURSELF, 'THE UNIVERSE SUPPORTS ME.'
- BREATHE IN THE POWER OF THE UNIVERSAL LIFE FORCE AND KNOW THAT EVERYTHING IS TAKEN CARE OF AND THAT YOU ARE SAFE.
- KEEP CHECKING THAT YOUR SHOULDERS ARE DOWN (THEY RISE WHEN YOU ARE FEELING STRESSED IN ANY WAY).
- ENJOY YOUR DAY OFF AND TRY IT AGAIN TOMORROW.
- THE UNIVERSE SUPPORTS YOU EVERY DAY; GET INTO THE HABIT OF REMEMBERING THIS.

Knowing If It's Love

Love means that you can be angry, say how you feel, voice your opinion, go around with no make-up and hairy legs, without worrying about being criticised or abandoned.

DENISE KNOWLES,
RELATE COUNSELLOR

When clients talk to me about their love problems, they sometimes say that they aren't sure whether to stay or to leave their relationship. Perhaps they have just met someone and don't know whether to invest their time and effort in making it work, or maybe they have been in a partnership for a while and feel that they are stuck in a relationship rut. And then there are those who have been unhappy with a man for years and are still trying to change him.

When our love lives get difficult, it is far too easy to get lost in nit-picking and criticism, even though we know that blame is never a problem-solving tool. In fact, as soon as we start to complain about all his faults, we have lost the ability to take charge of our own feelings and to understand what is really going on between us. And understanding is always the key to clarifying and resolving difficult relationship issues. So whatever the dilemma, I always take the client back to the basics of coaching, because this method opens up a positive and dynamic way forward.

The love coaching approach offers a step-by-step plan to get the love you want. First, of course, you need to know what you want. It is quite amazing how many of us seem to just drop into a relationship without ever having considered what we want from it. Would we buy a house in this ultra-casual way, or a car? Or even a new outfit or a washing machine? Would we go for a new job without researching whether it was exactly right for us? Of course we wouldn't, but lust-madness and the euphoria of love hormones cloud our usual good judgement when it comes to love. At the same time that we want romance and the knight in shining armour stuff, we really know that we also need a lot more than this. So what can we do?

It is entirely possible to enjoy the romance of love while *at the same time* being aware of our longer-term needs. Up-to-date research reveals two vitally important points:

All love relationships go through the same phases. This information makes it possible for us to place our own relationship within the context of one of the five phases of love, which we will be looking at. Once we do this, we can begin to put our love problems in some sort of perspective. This makes it easier to focus on exactly what is happening and why.

Specific criteria are required for a lasting and nurturing relationship. We can check whether our relationship fulfils these criteria, and so become more realistic about our long-term prospects.

The five phases of love

Look at the five phases listed here and see if you can see which phase your relationship is in at the moment. Recognise the possible new challenges that may arrive with each new stage.

1 The honeymoon phase

This is the so-called 'bonking and behaving' phase, a phrase that says it all. We are blissfully and blindly euphoric. He can do no wrong in our eyes; we are in love with love. But, as we know, this feeling fades as the hormones subside, and we start to face the realities of the relationship. So we move into the conflict phase.

2 The conflict phase

Everyday life begins to intrude and we no longer always see his behaviour tinted with a rosy glow. Our differences emerge and a power struggle may begin. One moment he was the man of our dreams, the next we find ourselves arguing. This is a natural part of growing closer together. You can never be intimate until you get to know each other, and conflicts are bound to emerge, with both of you wanting to be 'right'.

3 The understanding/misunderstanding phase

There are two possibilities now: to keep fighting each other or to start talking about what you both want. If you can resolve your arguments without criticism and sarcasm, you are on your way to greater intimacy and understanding. If you stay together and just keep fighting without working things out, your relationship will not be able to grow in a healthy way.

4 The stuck-in-a-rut phase

You are still together and are less in conflict. Things are easier but they might just start to get boring. This is a dangerous phase, when you can start to take each other for granted. *Routine* is the key word here. The passion may have been lost in the daily domestic round. You need to keep the fireworks popping. Get romantic and sexy and revive those feelings that you had on your first dates. Don't let familiarity breed contempt; let it breed greater intimacy.

5 The good team phase

You have come through the 'stuck' phase and breathed new life into your relationship. It takes two to achieve this, so now you know that both you and your partner are committed to the partnership. You have been through it and come out the other side, and this gives you both confidence and a strong feeling of security. You are in it for the long haul and you know that this is love!

So before you decide to ditch your relationship, just check which phase you find yourself in. Note the particular

INSTANT TIP

WHAT GOES AROUND COMES AROUND

THIS MEANS THAT YOU REAP WHAT YOU SOW, OR IN OTHER WORDS, YOU GET BACK WHAT YOU GIVE. WE HAVE SEEN HOW THIS WORKS IN RELATIONSHIPS: WE ATTRACT WHAT WE RADIATE, AND OTHERS REFLECT OUR INNER-MOST QUALITIES BACK TO US. TAKE THIS SIMPLE TRUTH AND USE IT TO ENLIVEN AND BRIGHTEN YOUR LOVE LIFE.

- IF YOUR SEX LIFE IS FLAGGING, DON'T WAIT FOR HIM TO TAKE THE INITIATIVE; GET SEXY AND SEDUCE HIM! GIVE HIM WHAT YOU WANT HIM TO GIVE YOU.
- YOU WISH HE WAS MORE ROMANTIC? SET THE SCENE. LIGHT THE CANDLES AND HAVE A SEXY GET-TOGETHER. ACT ROMANTICALLY AND YOU WILL ATTRACT ROMANCE.
- HE ISN'T TAKING ANY NOTICE OF YOUR FEELINGS? GET SUPER-SENSITIVE TO HIS EMOTIONAL NEEDS. ONCE HE FEELS THAT YOU HAVE HIS BEST INTERESTS AT HEART, YOUR RELATIONSHIP CAN MOVE UP A NOTCH AND HE WILL REALISE THAT YOU CAN BOTH GAIN FROM TALKING ABOUT YOUR FEELINGS.

STOP COMPLAINING ABOUT WHAT YOU WANT AND TRY *GIVING IT* INSTEAD; YOU WILL BE SURPRISED BY THE RESPONSE.

challenges that come with each stage and ask yourself how the two of you are handling them. Are you both prepared to work through the issues? True love is about being there for each other through thick and thin; it's about being self-aware and also being sensitive to your partner, and it's a two-way process. If one person is doing all the work, it is not a loving relationship, and if you are in emotional pain, it definitely isn't love!

Happy couples

What does being in a loving relationship mean to you? Is it great sex, emotional closeness, shared interests, good communication and similar goals? Or is it more to do with the luck of the draw or how much work you are prepared to put into it? The Enrich Couple Inventory was used in an important US study of married couples. The researchers took a sample of 21,501 couples (some who were happy together and others who were not) and asked them 195 intimate questions about their relationship.

The study revealed that a few key elements were common to all the relationships between couples who managed to stay together and overcome their life problems or difficult circumstances. Happy couples were good communicators. They had shared goals and were sexually compatible. They were flexible in handling differences, had a good balance of time spent together and apart, and could make joint financial decisions.

There are no surprises here, are there? If a relationship

is going to be good, it must have some key ingredients, and the couple must be committed to each other and prepared to work things out.

EXERCISE:

Are you happy together?

Look at the following diagram and give your relationship a score from one to ten for each of the six main happiness indicators.

1 = very poor
5 = average
10 = excellent

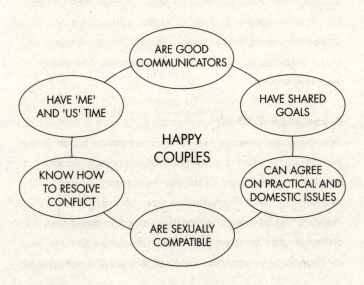

If you scored 6–19

You don't need me to tell you that your relationship is dying on its feet. Before you finally give up all hope, spend some time thinking about why these indicators are not present in your relationship. Which area needs the most attention? Where could you both do some work to kick-start your love life and get it back into gear again? If you both want to make a go of it, there is plenty of hope for you, because you are sharing a major goal and demonstrating your commitment. Make some effort to improve things or this relationship will fizzle away.

If you scored 20–29

Still not a very impressive score, but it could be worse! Your relationship is below average in the happiness stakes, and if it is to survive, you must do something quickly. Ask your partner what he thinks about the state of things between you. If he agrees that things could be better, you could begin a shared plan of action to improve things. This would be a major breakthrough for you both as you commit to saving your relationship.

If you scored 30–42

You are above average in the happiness stakes, which means you are doing some things right. Look at the indicators on which you scored high. What are the strengths in your relationship? Now where do you score badly? Which particular issues need attention? Focus on improving the communication between you – this is always the starting point for change. Give your love life some thought and energy and you will reap great rewards. This score may reflect a relationship that has fallen into the stuck-in-a-rut phase. It's time to recharge your batteries and get those sparks going again.

If you scored 43–60

If you are at the lower end of this score, there is still some work to be done, but you are well aware of this. Take the initiative and bear in mind the Instant Tip on page 201. Put into the relationship whatever you want out of it. Your partner is sensitive and aware and will respond to your overtures, so go to it! And many congratulations if you have a high score. You are both conscious of what it takes to keep the flame alive, and you are committed to the relationship and to each other. But you also know that relationships always need working on, because large doses of TLC are required if they are to stay vibrant and buzzing, so keep up the good work.

Communicating with each other

As part of the research for this book I ran my own Love Survey on the Internet. One of the participants in this survey responded, 'If only he would talk to me more and really listen to me when I talk to him. I feel as if I can't get through to him and it leaves me feeling alone and neglected. If we were communicating, we would be closer; as it is, I can feel us drifting further and further apart.' Over 75 per cent of the 329 people who took part said that communication was the most problematic issue in their love lives. We discussed this delicate subject in Chapter 6, so if you need to, just refresh your memory on the tips and strategies. Various respondents to the Love Survey suggested that when partners know how to communicate with each other they are more able to resolve any difficulties that emerge in their relationship. If either of you are unable to express your needs and emotions or feel that the other partner cannot really 'hear' what you are saying, the relationship is in danger. Ongoing unresolved communication issues lead either to relationship breakdown or to relationship resignation.

'Relationship resignation' is a term I started to use a few years ago to describe the way that so many long-term partnerships become stuck at a point where one or both of the participants *give up* on having their needs met within their relationship. This is an utterly tragic waste, because when you settle for less than you need, you are telling yourself that this is all you deserve. If you find yourself in this situation right now, take action and get to work to try to straighten things out between you and your partner. Use the techniques in this book to revitalise your love life. Never give up and accept second best, because you deserve the *very* best!

Having shared goals

In life coaching we are always concentrating on goals because they focus our energy and clarify what it is that we really want. In love coaching you can do exactly the same thing, and of course if your partner shares your relationship goals, you make a strongly motivated and committed team. For example, if you are climbing the career ladder and don't want to start a family for at least ten years, it's important that your partner knows this and is in agreement. This sounds obvious, but you would be amazed how many couples get together without knowing each other's plans, or (and perhaps worse still) they know that their plans are in potential conflict but hope that the other partner will eventually change their mind. This situation can lead to great emotional discord as well as creating an ongoing feeling of insecurity between you.

Elaine, 33, and Ian, 36, were both teachers at the same inner-city comprehensive. They moved into a flat together and eventually decided to get married. Elaine had always wanted to move out of town eventually and settle somewhere quieter. Ian knew this, but he loved city life and was certain that he would never want to leave. Each hoped the other would change. When Elaine became pregnant, she said that she wanted to move. This caused uproar between Elaine and Ian. Elaine reports feeling 'pulled apart' by the conflict. Ian eventually felt so pressurised and guilt-ridden that he applied for a teaching job in a small market town, although by this time both partners were feeling trapped. He was offered the job, but by now Elaine felt so guilty that she told him not to take it. She said she would rather stay in the city than have Ian be so unhappy. Their relationship never recovered, and when the baby was about two, Elaine left Ian and went to live in Cornwall.

I wonder what would have happened if they had thrashed out this difference before they got married. It doesn't do to go into a relationship hoping that the other person will change their mind over some big issue, because this rarely happens. And if one partner feels forced to climb down over something that is very important to them, they will never feel quite the same way about the relationship again.

When we embark on a committed love relationship, we make a deal with our partner, and there are various conditions attached. This might seem terribly unromantic, but it is the reality of the situation. You will never both agree on everything, but before you make a commitment to each other you need to share your opinions on many topics. For example, the Enrich Inventory revealed that if couples were to be happy, they had to see eye to eye over financial issues.

Practical considerations are very important when you are considering a permanent relationship. Where do you both want to live? Does he want children? Do you want children? What are his domestic habits like? Are you going to share household chores? Do you share the same values? And what about your spending and saving habits? Do they synchronise? All these things and more need to be thought about and potential differences aired *before* you become a permanent item. This doesn't mean that you should allow petty lifestyle differences to come between you, but *never* go into denial about big disagreements (hoping that he will change), because this will inevitably lead to conflict.

Your ideal man

If you are in a relationship with a man who is wrong for you, no amount of trying harder to communicate and understand each other will lead to long-term love. Many of us know to our cost that a gorgeous pair of chocolate-brown eyes or a body to rival Brad Pitt's will not sustain a relationship. Superficial characteristics may attract you in the first place (you lusted after him), but if he hasn't got the must-have ingredients, it won't ever be love.

EXERCISE:

Your top five must-haves

Imagine your ideal partner and think about all the qualities, abilities and characteristics that you would like him to have. Don't worry about being realistic at this stage; just put down whatever comes to mind. If you are short of ideas, take a look at the following example list to help you get started:

He must:
Be high in self-esteem
Love children and want children
Be positive
Appreciate me
Show his generosity
Share domestic chores
Be financially solvent

Be able to listen to me
Have good social skills
Get on with my friends
Be intelligent
Love sex and be good in bed
Be kind
Not be a flirt
Want a monogamous relationship
Be fairly attractive
Not be overweight
Be adventurous and spontaneous
Be interested in the arts
Be about my age or only a few years older
Like to travel
Not smoke

Once you have your list put a 'V' for vital or a 'D' for desirable next to each item. Now make a list of all the vital qualities in order of priority. Take the top five of this list and you will have your vital credentials.

Obviously, things change and nothing is set in stone. Our values alter, and what we once found highly desirable in a mate may not seem so important any more, so keep up to date with your top five must-haves. Be aware of this list when you are next attracted to a man. Check out his qualities. Does he fit in with your vital requirements? If he doesn't, why are you even considering him as a prospective partner?

Vanessa is 43 and has been divorced for three years. She was married to a man who was critical and hurtful. She left him once their child had gone to university. She was on her own and feeling very lonely when she met Sean, 56, a retired chartered accountant, at a friend's dinner party. At first, as he showered her with attention, she felt flattered, and all her friends were encouraging her to go out with him. He was intelligent and sharp but could also be quite waspish and nasty about other people, and Vanessa didn't like this side of his character. She had a relationship with him for a few months, but when he wanted to make it more permanent she decided to stop seeing him completely. She says, 'I was once married to a critical and spiteful man, and I decided when I left that I would never put up with that sort of behaviour again. The quality I most value in a man is kindness; this comes first for me now. I nearly moved in with Sean because it was so great to be part of a couple again, but when it came down to it, I knew it wouldn't work. Sean has many qualities, but kindness is not one of them, so I knew I had to end it before I got involved in another disastrous relationship.'

Of course, we have to be realistic about people; we can't expect them to be perfect, but we do have to be aware of our own needs. If a man does not demonstrate a quality that you know is vital to you, let this be a warning. If your essential needs are not being met, this relationship is not a loving one for you. You can choose who to love. Choose well!

Sexual compatibility

US relationship therapist Michele Weiner-Davis, who has written a book called *The Sex-Starved Marriage*, believes that 'sex-starved' relationships are becoming commonplace. In fact, she states that, 'An estimated one in three couples struggle with low sexual desire.' An Internet survey for netdoctor.co.uk supports her findings, with statistics showing that only 30 per cent of those in long-term relationships feel they are having enough sex.

A good sex life is a vital element of a loving and lasting relationship. Sex is not the only thing that's important, but it enhances communication and intimacy levels and creates a powerful bond between you. If one partner feels sexually deprived, there will be trouble! The Enrich Inventory revealed that nearly a third of unhappy couples named their sex life as a source of dissatisfaction and conflict. Of course, if things are not going so well outside the bedroom, this will naturally affect our sex life. Women often tell me that if only their partner would become closer emotionally, they would feel more sexual towards him! So sex, communication and emotional closeness are all part of the intimacy package.

Once we are in a long-term relationship, sex can become less exciting, and if we are to keep the flame burning amidst domesticity, childcare and all life's other demands, we need to make a concerted effort. Again, it comes back to communication. If we can talk about our sex lives to each other, we are more likely to keep our love alive.

Ten sex tips for a loving long-term relationship

1 Talk about it. If you have lost the lust in your relationship, start looking for it again. Talk to each other about what is happening (or isn't happening). Why is your sex life flagging? Perhaps you are both too tired or stressed. If so, plan a quiet night together and spend time discussing your feelings. You will find that this makes you feel much closer to each other.

2 Make an effort to re-create your dating days. Make a date with each other and meet at the venue. Act as if you are really dating and you will be amazed by how different this feels. It's very easy to take each other for granted. Never do this; it can lead to much heartbreak. If you want your relationship to feel fresh and vibrant, you must keep it sexually alive.

3 Communicate your sexual needs. Talk about sex to each other. This in itself is a fabulous turn-on. Let go of your inhibitions and get down to it. Show him what you like and ask him what he likes and you will be greatly gratified by the response. The more you think about sex, the sexier you will feel, so get started. Why not take a trip together to Ann Summers and buy some sex toys?

4 Keep the romance alive. If you have romance, your sex life will stay buzzing. How can you fancy each other if you don't make an effort to make the other one feel special? You are not the only one who wants to feel desired; he needs to feel wanted too. Show him how much you want him. Put away your usual nightwear and get out something a bit more glamorous. Men are aroused by erotic lingerie, so why not get some? He will be over the moon, and you will be surprised by the wonderful effect this has on you too. Come on! Let out that inner sex goddess and give your sex life a well deserved boost. If it needs you to make that first step, then do it. Your relationship might be at stake.

5 Think about sex all day. It's madness to think that after a long hard day you will both be longing for sex. You are far more likely to long for sleep. So keep up the anticipation all day by making suggestive phone calls, leaving love notes around the house, sending saucy emails and texts and generally keeping the hormones buzzing. By the time you meet up again, you will be ready for each other.

6 Do it differently. If your partner usually initiates sex, try changing roles. If you usually take the lead, back off and suggest that you have sexual contact but no intercourse for a week (this will get the juices going in erotic anticipation). Light candles and burn scented oils in your bedroom and turn it into a sexy venue. And why always do it at night in bed? Try an early morning tryst in the bathroom (before the children get up, if necessary). Get out of your rut, change your routines and bring back the excitement of the unknown and different. Both of you will be delighted. Your relationship is worth it!

7 Give each other sexual surprises. The average couple only ever use three positions: woman on top, missionary and 'doggy-style'. Buy a sex guide and discover lots of different ways to do it. Try role-playing and acting out fantasies. Arrange a surprise date and keep each other on your toes. Bring back that lustful hormone-induced high that you both so used to enjoy.

8 Keep it light. A good sense of humour is a great turn-on. Be positive, upbeat and supportive with your partner. Make each other laugh, and stop taking life (even your sex life) too seriously.

9 Give each other plenty of TLC. Make lots of physical contact throughout the day. Kiss, cuddle, hold hands and flirt outrageously with him. Remind him how much you fancy him (he needs to be told). Build towards the sexual act by being sexual with each other even in everyday situations.

10 Be sexually confident. Follow your instincts and don't let embarrassment hinder you. Act out the sexual predator with your partner and see what this feels like. Explore this part of your character and enjoy your sexuality. Sex, like everything else in life, needs attention if it is to thrive. Throw yourself into revitalising the sexual side of your relationship and just watch your love life blossom.

Love is knowing how to resolve conflict.

Film actress Simone Signoret says: 'Chains do not hold a marriage together. It is threads, hundreds of tiny threads, which sew people together through the years.' My parents have been happily married for fifty-five years and as time goes by I become more and more intrigued by the strategies they use to create these 'threads'. There is no doubt that successful love relationships depend upon a complex mix of sexual chemistry, mutual appreciation, and the desire and ability to resolve conflict when it arises.

An outstanding difference between grumpy couples and happy couples lies in the way they approach conflict. Some happy couples might enjoy a good row, but they always know when to draw a line under it and move on.

INSTANT TIP

YOU KNOW IT'S LOVE WHEN . . .

- YOU STILL TURN EACH OTHER ON.
- HE IS YOUR BEST FRIEND.
- YOU HAVE A REALISTIC VIEW OF YOUR RELATIONSHIP.
- YOU CAN FORGIVE EACH OTHER'S MISTAKES.
- YOU ARE BOTH PREPARED TO WORK AT YOUR RELATIONSHIP.
- YOU CAN TRUST HIM.
- HE FOLLOWS THROUGH AND IS RELIABLE.
- YOU CAN IMAGINE BEING TOGETHER IN OLD AGE.
- YOU RESPECT EACH OTHER.
- YOU CAN HAVE A ROW AND CLEAR THE AIR AND THEN LET IT GO AND MOVE ON.
- HE APPRECIATES YOU AND SHOWS IT.
- YOU APPRECIATE HIM AND SHOW IT.
- YOU STILL MAKE AN EFFORT FOR EACH OTHER.

Anyone in a long-term relationship will know that conflict is inevitable, so possessing a set of workable strategies is an absolute necessity. I have watched both my parents stepping delicately around each other over certain issues. They have learned what to say (and when to say it) and what not to say, and they both have an immaculate sense of timing. We acquire these skills as our relationship develops. They are some of the 'tiny threads' that we sew together. Living with perpetual disagreement drains all the love from a relationship; it makes us tired, resentful and depressed and leads to total communication breakdown. So what can happy loving couples teach us about conflict resolution? I asked a number of people in long-term relationships for their tips. These are some of the things they suggested:

- When you are about to lose your temper, take ten (or more) deep breaths.
- Choose your moment carefully if you want to talk about something controversial. Find a time when you are both relaxed and in a good mood.
- If you are in total disagreement, stop talking and agree to sleep on it (this shows an awareness of the other's point of view).
- Arguing over petty grievances often masks deeper issues. Check whether this is the case. Perhaps he is really going mad because his sexual needs aren't being met. Or maybe you are furious with him because he isn't listening to you? Clear up the big issues and the minor rows will disappear like magic.

- Be flexible and considerate towards your partner. Sometimes it will be necessary to make concessions and to accept that he cannot always be perfect. If he has your vital must-have qualities, you must be prepared to accept some minor irritating personality traits (we all have them). If he's generous and sexy but untidy, maybe you will have to decide to appreciate the good things and put up with the mess. If he's kind and a wonderful father, you might have to overlook the fact that he never remembers your wedding anniversary or loves to watch football all weekend. Face it: you will never find a man with every single quality you could wish for, so be ready to make some allowances. And remember that he will be doing this too, when he discovers your little idiosyncrasies.

- Never use critical statements when talking to a loved one. This will only make more problems; it will never build bridges. Own your own feelings. For example, instead of staying, 'Why don't you ever help with domestic work?' say, 'When you don't help in the house I feel taken for granted.' It's not what you say but how you say it that makes all the difference.

- Let the other partner be right sometimes. This is a really great tip and one I use often. Agree with him on some minor issue: yes, he is right! He will be disarmed and much more approachable next time (when the issue might be bigger).

In life coaching we look at our preferred outcome and work out ways to achieve it. Use this strategy in your relationships. How can you get what you want? What is the best and most diplomatic approach? Learn to accommodate your partner's needs along with your own. Negotiate with style and grace, and your loved one will appreciate you for it (and you are much more likely to get your own way!).

Love means having the right balance of 'me' and 'us' time

Remember your dating days. What fascinated you about each other? When you met you brought two lives together, and this enriched the relationship. Don't ever give up your own interests, friendships and goals when you get together with a partner. Some couples get so bound up in each other during the infatuation phase that they give up their social lives and exist just to be with each other. But this phase doesn't last. If and when you move into a long-term relationship, it is vital that you have your own life as well as a life with your partner. It's important to maintain a sense of self within your relationship so that you remain confident and independent. Remember that a love magnet does her own thing. This allows her to feel free and positive and enhances her love relationships.

The Enrich Inventory (see page 202) found that happy couples had a good balance of leisure time spent together and apart. If he loves playing golf, then don't expect him to stop playing when you become an item. And how about your nights out with the girls? You won't want to lose contact with your friends. Loving couples allow each other some freedom, and this can only improve the relationship.

A good partnership also benefits from time spent together doing fun activities. You could join an evening class together, start playing Bridge or take up cycling. The possibilities are endless. Making time for each other and sharing interests are just more ways of adding to the tiny threads that sew you together through the years.

EXERCISE:

Is it love?

Decide the status of your relationship. Is it love? Could it be love? Or is it going nowhere? Read each of the following statements and ask yourself if they are true for your relationship. Score as follows:

1 almost never
2 sometimes
3 often
4 almost always

1 I am pleased by the way that my partner and I communicate with each other.
2 He knows when I need time and attention and is prepared to give it to me.

3 We talk openly about our sex life.

4 We agree over how much to spend and how much to save.

5 We spend quality time together.

6 We both have our own interests and friends.

7 Our relationship is very close.

8 I am happy with the way that we share the domestic workload.

9 He is kind and thoughtful.

10 We tolerate each other's annoying habits.

11 I appreciate him.

12 He appreciates me.

13 If we argue we know how to cool off and resolve the situation.

14 We show our commitment to each other.

15 I would describe our relationship as intimate.

If you scored 15–24

Well, you are still together in spite of the difficulties! Issues need to be faced, but you don't need me to tell you this. You are feeling stretched by this relationship and desperately need to make changes. The key here is to find out if your partner feels the same. Is he also troubled by the way things are going? You could ask him to do this exercise and see what score he comes up with. If you both feel that you have a problem, there is hope for your relationship, as you can work together to make things better. If he believes that everything is fine (or he doesn't care anyway), maybe you need to have a big think about exactly where this relationship is going.

If you scored 25–34

Some things are working in your relationship, so this is good news. Look at the statements on which you scored highest and think about what it's like when you work in harmony with each other. Now look at where you scored badly. Why are there difficulties here? Ask your partner to do this exercise and then discuss both sets of answers. Show him that you want to make the relationship work and see how he reacts. There are already some strong features in your partnership, and you can build on these. If you can both make a commitment to some relationship goals, you have a great chance of being successful.

If you scored 35–44

You both know how to make your relationship work, and your score could be even higher. Exactly how can you turn those 'sometimes' answers into 'often'? And what would it take for you to turn the 'often' answers into 'almost always'? Get together and congratulate yourself on your score. Your relationship has a lot going for it. Now how can you make it even better? Set some new relationship goals together and create an action plan that will help you to achieve them. Work on your relationship; it is worth it!

If you scored 45–60

It's love! You are in a wonderful relationship, but of course you know this. You are both aware that it takes two to keep a love relationship alive and flourishing, and you both know how to play your part. Congratulations!

MEDITATION MOMENT

APPRECIATING YOUR PARTNER

Sit quietly and think about your loved one. Can you remember how you felt when you first met? When did you realise that you were attracted to him? Think back to some of your early dates. Visualise them and remember your feelings. Get into those feelings and appreciate how much he turned you on!

Now reflect on your relationship and think of some past times when your partner showed his love for you. Remember how you felt. Get into those feelings again.

Now think of ten things that you appreciate about him and write them down.

I . . . (name) . . . appreciate you . . . (his name) for . . . .

Show your partner this list when you have finished. Pin it up somewhere so that you are reminded to appreciate his finer qualities. The more you appreciate him, the more he will appreciate you. It takes two to make love happen.

Bouncing Back from Heartbreak

Heartbreak is caused by the end of a relationship. It can also be caused when we fail to get a relationship we fervently desire. It can even happen slowly when we realise that we are in a relationship from which all the love has gone.

PAUL MCKENNA

Nicole and Tom, Diana and Charles, and Jerry and Mick are just a few of the many high-profile marriage break-ups that we have watched unfold under the unforgiving media spotlight. And all the rest of us who have endured the emotional pain of heartbreak can at least be glad that we were spared the humiliation of the public gaze. It's bad enough to go through this process in the privacy of your own home, but to be watched and judged as you do so must be total agony.

Neither wealth, fame, talent, beauty nor status can cushion us from heartbreak; nothing can stop us suffering the intense emotional pain that comes at the end of a love relationship. We fall in love and in the best tradition of romantic novels and fairytales we expect a happy-ever-after ending. But real life brings surprises and change and relationship break-ups. Most of us will have had our hearts broken at least once, and some will have experienced this many times. We all know the pain that comes with the parting of the ways.

Whether you had been together a few weeks, a few months or many years, and whether you ended it or he did, the feelings may well be difficult to handle. When we open our lives to another person and become intimate, we also admit our vulnerability and need. This is all part of getting close to a loved one. If and when the ending comes, there will be a natural feeling of loss and separation, along with a whole host of other difficult emotions that we shall look at in a moment.

If you are going through a break-up right now, it will probably feel like the end of the world – and in a way it is. It's the end of the world as you have known it and the beginning of a whole new way of life (possibly a scary thought). When I tell you that it will get better and that you will survive this, I know you will find it hard to believe me. But it's true; *this too shall pass!* I promise that you will recover and live to tell the tale, but it might take a while.

There are only two ways to go:

1 You can try to 'protect' yourself by denying your feelings. Our natural reaction is to push the pain away, a defensive measure to help us to get over our shock and disorientation. This way doesn't work in the long term, because eventually these difficult emotions will surface (probably when you least expect them to) and you will have to deal with them.

2 You can face up to your emotions, feel them and heal them. This is the way that will allow you to let go and move forward. Healing always brings new insights and awareness and a fresh vibrant energy which helps you to accept the past and create a brand new future.

Emma, 26, a stylist, had been dating George, 29, for a few months. They made a good-looking couple, and everyone said what a perfect match they were. They had an exciting social life and a great sex life, and Emma was pretty sure that he was the right man for her. George worked for a high-powered advertising agency and was a real super-achiever. They both had their separate interests and only saw each other once or twice in the week and at weekends. One night Emma was out for dinner with a girlfriend when she saw George at another table with a glamorous woman. She was utterly shocked and changed seats so that he wouldn't see her. As the night wore on, it became obvious that they were on a romantic date, and when they left she went home devastated.

After a sleepless night Emma phoned George to confront him, but he was just bemused by her attitude. He told her that he saw other women when they weren't together but that he thought that was part of their arrangement and that of course she was free to do the same. Emma was shattered as she faced the end of her romantic dream about the two of them. She felt as if she had been taken for an idiot and lost all her confidence in herself. For a few days she just hid away feeling like a victim and was not able to face up to anything. She says, 'At first, after I came home that night, I convinced myself that I had made a mistake (maybe she was his sister?). I just couldn't believe that he would treat me like that. And then I felt totally let down and mistrustful, but I also missed him. One moment I was longing to see him and then suddenly I would feel really furious with him. I was totally confused and I couldn't keep my life together; it felt like everything was falling apart. Then my friend Liz came round and we talked for a long time. I realised that he and I had been having a different relationship. I was fantasising about a big white wedding and he was just playing the field. I rang him and told him we were finished. He was surprised and offered to take me out for a drink, but by then I knew it was never going to be what I had imagined. I spent the next six months feeling uncomfortable and low in self-esteem, and I lost trust in men and in my own decision-making powers. But eventually I came through it and out the other end. It was a long haul, but afterwards I felt like I understood myself better. I knew that I had become more realistic about myself, my life and my relationships.'

Confusion, mixed emotions, denial, anger, hopelessness, loss of self-esteem, you name it . . . you feel all this and more when a relationship in which you invested your emotions has ended. When I separated from my first husband, I remember a curious mixture of elation, fury, guilt and depression. I could swing in and out each of these states in a few seconds. I remember feeling out of control of my emotions and out of control of my life for quite a long time before I settled into a more accepting frame of mind. It was not an easy time, and I didn't know then what I knew now: namely, that I would go through a roller-coaster of emotions and I would have to come to terms with them before I could let go of the painful loss of my precious marriage.

INSTANT TIP

WHY A BOX OF CHOCOLATES MIGHT HELP!

EARLIER WE LOOKED AT THE ROLE OF THE CHEMICAL PEA, WHICH HELPS TO INDUCE THE AMAZING LOVER'S HIGH THAT WE FEEL AT THE BEGINNING OF A RELATION-SHIP. THE EXISTENCE OF PEA EXPLAINS WHY WE CRAVE LOVE AND ALSO WHY A RELATIONSHIP THAT ENDS IN THE EARLY STAGES CAN BE SO PAINFUL TO BEAR.

NEUROPHYSIOLOGISTS IN NEW YORK STUDYING THE BRAIN CHEMISTRY OF LOVE DISCOVERED THAT AT THE END OF AN AFFAIR THE BRAIN DRASTICALLY REDUCES THE PRODUCTION OF PEA, CAUSING FEELINGS OF DEPRESSION AND STRESS. SO IF YOUR LIFE FEELS EMPTY WHEN YOUR RELATIONSHIP GOES WRONG, IT MAY WELL BE THAT YOU ARE SUFFERING FROM WITHDRAWAL SYMPTOMS. AND IF YOU HAVE FOUND YOURSELF TURNING TO CHOCOLATE, YOU ARE PROBABLY ONLY TRYING TO RAISE YOUR PEA LEVELS.

CHOCOLATE CONTAINS STIMULANT CHEMICALS THAT

ARE SIMILAR TO PEA, AND IT HAS BEEN SUGGESTED
THAT CHOCOLATE BINGEING MAY BE A FORM OF 'SELF-
MEDICATION' TO COMPENSATE FOR THE LOSS OF THE
LOVER'S HIGH. SO IN THE SHORT TERM A CHOCOLATE
TREAT MIGHT WELL BE EXACTLY WHAT YOU NEED.

IF YOU HAVE JUST BEEN DUMPED, TRY TO BEAR IN
MIND THAT THE END-OF-THE-WORLD FEELING HAS AS
MUCH TO DO WITH PEA WITHDRAWAL AS ANYTHING
ELSE. THIS MAY HELP TO GIVE YOU SOME PERSPECTIVE.

AND WHAT A GREAT EXCUSE FOR A (MEDICINAL) BOX
OF BELGIAN CHOCS!

The five stages of emotional healing

Life brings joy and pain, meetings and partings, endings
and fresh starts, loss and gain, and we have to deal with
all that it brings. 'Bouncing back' wonderfully describes
our capacity to go into a dark place only to eventually rise
back up again with renewed purpose. If you are in the
throes of a painful break-up, you need to know that nature
has given you an inbuilt foolproof method to deal with
your loss; it's called the grieving process. Yes I know that
we usually talk about grieving in relation to death, but in
grief counselling it is recognised that we react to all loss
in the same way. The grieving process allows us gradually
to let go of our attachment to people, places or even
dreams that never came true.

Take a look at the stages listed below, bearing in mind that they don't necessarily happen in order and that you can jump around from one stage to another at any time. For example, you might go from being in denial one moment to feeling full of anger the next, or maybe you start to feel afraid of the future and then find yourself doubting the reality of what has happened. These stages are a natural part of the healing process, and the very best thing you can do is let them run their course rather than trying to fight your feelings.

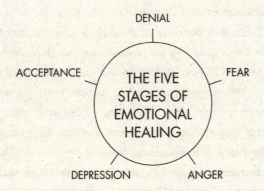

Stage 1: Denial

Shock brings denial. You cannot believe it is really over. It can't be true, can it? Surely we will get back together. This may develop so that instead of feeling miserable you are just waiting for it to be OK again – he has packed his bags and moved out and you *still* think you are just having a break from each other. You look back at how great everything was and torment yourself with happy memories.

Maybe you feel numb and disconnected from your life. Nothing matters and you couldn't care less about anything. Perhaps you start bargaining with the universe, suggesting things that you will do or ways in which you will change *if only* it will all come right again.

If you are in denial, do this: Let yourself feel the shock and numbness. Sit it out. Talk to a close friend who has a big listening ear. Recognise that you are in denial and wait until it passes. Don't worry, it will!

Stage 2: Fear

It feels like the end of all your dreams. Will you ever feel better? What will become of you? How can life carry on now that he is gone? Is there anybody out there who is just for you? Will you be left on the shelf? How will you ever have the confidence to date again? You can never trust another man . . . etc., etc. Yes, you will get everything out of proportion for a while as you face negativity and disillusionment.

If you are feeling afraid, do this: Talk to an understanding friend who will remind you that your fears are not grounded in reality. Your negative thoughts will pass. Just feel the fear and you will be able to let go and move on.

Stage 3: Anger

Anger is an absolutely natural reaction, but one that we sometimes suppress for various reasons. Unexpressed anger is very bad for you, so face it even if it makes you uncomfortable. You might be mad at him for not being the man you thought he was. You might be furious with yourself for not seeing things clearly. You might just be in a wild hopping fury about everything!

If you are feeling angry, do this: Choose an appropriate time and place to shout and scream. Beat the hell out of a feather pillow. Get physical – go for a run, a swim, a bike ride, a walk . . . and let that energy out! Talk to someone if this helps.

Stage 4: Depression

Everything feels pointless. Is it worth ever getting out of bed again? If there is a black cloud hanging over you, try to hold on to the knowledge that it has a silver lining and that you will get to see it once the bad times have passed. It's hard to see any joy in the world when you are in despair, but remember, *this feeling will pass*.

If you are feeling depressed, do this: Get under the duvet with a pile of mags and a box of chocolates if they help. In other words, give yourself lots of TLC and do whatever it takes to nurture and comfort yourself. Seek professional help if you need to.

Stage 5: Acceptance

You have been on an emotional treadmill and now you are ready to get off. Whatever happened is in the past. It is over and done with. You learned a lot from the relationship and now you are ready to let go of the old and embrace the new.

When you can accept it, do this: Recognise how much you have changed while going through the grieving process (whether it took three days, three weeks or three years). You have healed the hurt inside you and this will make you stronger and more resilient in the future. Bounce back into life and love, and appreciate your brilliance and stamina!

But it hurts too much!

In life coaching we often suggest that you 'fake it till you make it', and this is certainly a good short-term tactic, as it boosts our confidence and helps us to carry on as usual (whatever is going on in our emotional lives). But painful emotions cannot be healed in this way, and there will come a time in a relationship break-up when you need to get real about what you are feeling.

During the first few months of my separation I couldn't bear the prospect of facing my feelings, so I filled my life with practical details and 'just got on with it' (secretly hoping that this would work). It didn't, of course, and there followed a string of health issues and negative states until I hit rock bottom and there was nothing to do except to acknowledge the depths of my feelings. They were not going to go away and I couldn't hide from them any more. If you are feeling uncomfortable right now because you know that you are sitting on some difficult emotions, please relax whilst I explain how easy it is for you to deal with them.

The most important thing to know is that *your feelings cannot hurt you*! It's true. The feelings themselves don't hurt; it is only our resistance that causes pain. Your feelings directly reflect your needs, so whenever you are denying what you feel, you are in effect denying your own needs. Now *that* hurts! You might be angry with your ex because you are now feeling low in self-confidence and self-respect. If you pretend that you are not angry (Oh, everything is fine; I can cope; he didn't mean to hurt me . . .), you are denying your need to regain your feelings of self-worth. And *the only way* to regain your power is to acknowledge and express your anger (in some suitable way). It's OK to be angry; in fact, it's quite natural. If you deny your feelings 'in case they hurt', you will get stuck in a negative place.

Your rainbow of emotions

Visualise this: you are surrounded by beautiful coloured bubbles. All the bubbles are different in size and colour, and they are floating around gently bumping into each other and then floating off in another direction. These bubbles represent the whole range of the emotional responses that you have experienced and are all the colours of the rainbow. They have a shimmering and translucent beauty, and each one is unique and conveys your emotional individuality.

Our emotions are a fascinating and natural expression of who we are and what we are going through, yet sometimes we are afraid of owning them. In childhood we are often taught that our feelings are best kept to ourselves in case:

- We are overwhelmed by them and lose control.
- We show our emotional 'weaknesses' and become vulnerable.
- We demonstrate our 'neediness'.
- We reveal our true self.

But the simple truth is that our feelings are related to our needs. And if our needs are fulfilled, we feel all right, and if they are not fulfilled, we don't feel all right. Although we may become practised in the art of hiding our feelings, they stick around regardless. *Hidden feelings don't go away*. They have to be concealed somewhere and so they pile up inside us and bring pain and misery.

Let's go back to those beautiful bubbles. Imagine that whenever you feel something you create a beautiful coloured bubble of that feeling around you. The emotion surrounds you. You might be experiencing something difficult like fear, anger or helplessness. The feeling is everywhere; it embraces you. Now what can you do? You can pretend it isn't there, but we know that won't work for long. The only way to dispel a particular emotional bubble is to *move through it*. This requires that you experience the *whole* bubble. You have to feel the feeling right through. The trick is to keep moving. Move along with the feeling; go where it takes you. The experience may be intense, but it will not cause you pain. Remember that feelings only hurt when you resist them.

Take the fear out of your feelings and *just feel them*. Look again at the five stages of emotional healing on page 231 and recognise if there is something you are not facing up to. The sooner you can allow yourself to feel things through, the sooner you can let go of your pain and leave heartbreak hotel – a happy and wiser woman!

EXERCISE:

Letting go

If you are struggling to face up to a feeling at the moment, try this simple process of letting go. Using your journal if you have one, complete the following statements in as much detail as is necessary.

I (name) . . am denying that I feel . . . .
I . . . . am denying that I feel . . . .
                 because . . . .
I . . . . am ready to accept that I feel . . . .
I . . . . accept that I feel . . . .
I . . . . love and value all my experiences.
I . . . . give myself permission to feel . . . .

You are now allowing yourself to experience the denied emotion. You may be having all sorts of associated feelings. Are you? If so, acknowledge these feelings. You could say them or write them down; just find a way to express all you are feeling at the moment. Do you feel guilty or angry with yourself? If so, take up your pen again and write:

I . . . . . . forgive myself.

Do you feel angry with anyone else? If so, write:

I . . . . . . forgive you . . . . . . (name of person).

All this forgiveness might make you feel even more anger. If so, stick with it and don't be afraid of the intensity of your feelings. *Your feelings cannot hurt you.* The greater the intensity of your feelings, the more you are letting go. If you are afraid of the depth of your feelings at any time during this exercise, just acknowledge and express your fear. You could write:

I . . . . . . am frightened of my feelings

Whenever you express your fear you will feel less frightened. Whenever you express your anger you will feel less angry. Whenever you express your guilt you will feel less guilty.

Writing your feelings is one way to express them. Other ways of private expression include speaking your written statements out loud. A very powerful way is to speak out loud into a mirror. Sounds a bit crazy? Try it. Try anything that may help you. If you are angry, get on to that feather pillow. If you are sad, let yourself cry.

There may come a time when you feel like sharing your feelings. Talking to someone who you trust may help. Perhaps you could use the letting go exercise and read your statements to the other person. And if you feel the need for some professional counselling support, get it!

Be flexible and allow yourself to experiment with your approach. Use whichever technique works for you. As you move from denial into acceptance, you will feel the positive effects in all areas of your life. You have learned a lot about yourself during your break-up and you can now move on in style, knowing that you are a woman with inner strength and determination and that you deserve a man who fully appreciates *all* your qualities.

Be your own cheerleader

Let's face it, you can only eat so much chocolate. Very soon self-medicating will start to border on over-indulgence and then it's time to stop eating and to start to support yourself – big time.

It's important to remember that your emotional healing will be an up-and-down process. Sometimes it might feel that you go one step forward only to take two steps back, and this can make you self-critical and negative. Give yourself a break! You are going through a massive change and coming to terms with challenging feelings, so don't make it even harder by blaming yourself.

Supporting yourself really means believing and trusting in yourself even when you are hurting (especially when you are hurting!). Self-criticism and negative judgements will only slow up the healing process, so just get on your own side. Stand by yourself and be your own biggest fan and best friend. Be your own cheerleader! There is no one whose encouragement and good opinion can mean more to you; self-worth and self-belief are the keys to your development. The healing process may take many twists and turns, but it always leads onwards and upwards. You may have a few good days and then find yourself steeped in fear and depression. This doesn't mean that you are a 'failure' or that you have 'lost control again'; it only means that something has come up that needs to be healed. Face this with optimism and know that you are always moving forwards.

Helen, 41, is a mother of three who has recently divorced John after a 20-year marriage. Helen and John had been drifting apart for more than ten years. Even though they tried couple counselling, they couldn't retrieve their marriage and so decided to split. Although it was Helen who initiated the proceedings, she did so with a heavy heart and has struggled to come to terms with her situation. She says that she was amazed by her often contradictory emotions and her ongoing feelings of vulnerability and fear. 'At first I was pleased with myself for having the confidence to go through with it all, but then I became self-doubting and I wondered whether to get back together with John (he would have come back at any time). I would go out with friends and feel adult and independent and then suddenly be overwhelmed by guilt and remorse and rush home early (much to the surprise of the babysitter). I also found it very hard to get to sleep and I would often wake up in a panic thinking that I was doing the wrong thing. But something inside me made me stick to my guns. Even when I was at my lowest, I knew I had to see this through. When the divorce papers finally arrived, I fell into a depression that felt like the pits. But after a couple of weeks the black cloud lifted and it has been getting lighter ever since. It would be no exaggeration to say that I feel like a different woman and my life has opened up in so many ways. It hasn't been easy, but I know I made the right choice, and deep inside I never seriously questioned if I was doing the right thing; I *knew* I was doing the right thing.'

INSTANT TIP

TRUST YOURSELF

THE ANSWERS TO ALL YOUR PROBLEMS LIE WITHIN YOU. TEMPTING THOUGH IT IS TO LOOK TO OUTSIDE AUTHORITY FIGURES (A CHILDHOOD HABIT) AND OTHER PEOPLE'S OPINIONS, THE BUCK STOPS WITH US. WE ARE THE GREATEST AUTHORITY ON OURSELVES; ALL WE NEED TO DO IS TRUST OUR OWN JUDGEMENT. THIS MIGHT FEEL HARD TO DO WHILE WE ARE IN THE THROES OF A BREAK-UP, BUT IT IS REALLY THE ONLY WAY TO REGAIN CONTROL.

START GIVING YOURSELF *FEELING CHECKS* THROUGHOUT THE DAY.

- EVERY NOW AND AGAIN ASK YOURSELF HOW YOU ARE FEELING.
- CHECK YOUR INTUITIVE RESPONSES TO WHATEVER IS GOING ON AROUND YOU. WHAT IS YOUR GUT

---

reaction? Don't think too much about this;
just go with your first feeling.

- If someone asks a favour, don't automatically say yes. Look at your feelings; would you rather say no?

- If you find yourself feeling uncomfortable in any situation, check out why this is.

- Notice when you are feeling victimised by someone. What are your feelings here? Act on them.

- Who is not treating you well? Be aware of their behaviour and how it affects you. What can you do about this?

- Get into the habit of checking things out with yourself. Ask: how do I feel about this? How will that impact on me? How do I feel about this person? What do I judge to be the best response? Am I doing the right thing?

- Remember that you can always trust yourself. When in doubt just slow down and ask your own advice, and then take it!

- Your inner wise woman is only a thought away!

Who loves you, baby?

Right now you need all the support and morale boosting you can lay your hands on, so it's time to check who is really on your side. Get clear about the people in your life. You need positive support and emotional (and possibly practical) help right now. The angels who supply this positive energy are called your *believing mirrors*, because they reflect your very best self. They mirror your own strong self-belief and confidence, and in doing so they remind you that, yes, you can get through this and come out smiling! Who are these angels in your life?

Sometimes when we are feeling low we find it hard to discriminate between *believing mirrors* and those who (intentionally or unintentionally) just drain our energy. These *energy vampires* bring us down with their negativity, cynicism and depression; they literally suck the life force from us and leave us feeling weak and dejected. You might think that we would have the sense to stay right away from such people, but when we are feeling somewhat negative ourselves, we tend to attract further negativity and even to start believing the very worst of our world and ourselves. If you are not sure who is good for you and who is bad for you, just try this simple test. Energy vampires leave you feeling worse about yourself, and believing mirrors leave you feeling better about yourself, so just start to notice who is having what effect on you. Here are a few defining characteristics:

BELIEVING MIRRORS	ENERGY VAMPIRES
Give support	Are cynical
Share their feelings	Believe the worst
Are optimistic	Talk about themselves a lot
Are positive	Are self-centred
Listen to you	Are not interested in you
Are light-hearted	Are pessimistic
Share your load	Leave you feeling worse
Are non-critical	Make judgements
Believe in you	Complain a lot
Leave you feeling better	Tell you what you 'should'
Want the best for you	or 'ought to' be doing

Now make a list of the people around you: friends, relatives, colleagues, and relatives and friends of your ex if you are involved with them. Write a list of all their names and then put 'BM' (for believing mirror) or 'EV' (for energy vampire) next to their name. Don't be shocked if there are some big surprises in there. EVs can sometimes appear to be BMs until you think about them clearly. Even if a close family member turns out to be an EV, *just stay away from them at the moment*. Later, when you are feeling more yourself, it will be possible to deal with them, but for now stick with your believing mirrors; they are the ones who will help to pull you through.

MEDITATION MOMENT

SEEING THE BIGGER PICTURE

Things are not always what they seem. When we start focusing on the detail, it's easy to lose the overview of a situation. In this meditation you give yourself the chance to stand aside for a moment and take a look at the bigger picture of your life.

- Imagine you are contemplating the whole of your life from beginning to end. You can see every single thing that has happened to you, why it happened and where it led you.

- Now think about your relationship from this vantage point and look for the deeper meaning and purpose behind it.

- Ask yourself such questions as: why did I go into this relationship? What has it taught me about myself? How have I changed since the break-up? What new lessons have I learned? How will my new awareness serve me in the future?

- Remember that things that seem 'negative' at first might actually be serving a purpose. For example, you can't meet Mr Right for You if you are still dating Mr Entirely Wrong for

You. And maybe you needed to learn lessons from dating Mr Wrong so that you can have a healthy relationship with Mr Right.

- In the future it will be easy to look back and understand the meaning and purpose behind your break-up, so why not tap into that understanding right now. It will help with your recovery.

- See the bigger picture and get the end of this relationship in perspective and then you will be ready to move on.

Loving Yourself

While you are in a relationship, it can sometimes feel as if the goal is to love your man as best you can so that he will be happy, and thus you will be happy. However, the true goal is to love yourself in good times and bad, no matter what.

MARNI KAMINS AND
JANICE MACLEOD

I want to let you in on a little secret, one that is vital to your success: even love magnets get the blues. Yes, it's true. Positive-thinking, go-getting girls; sex goddesses; self-believers – they all have their off-days. It isn't possible to be brimming with self-confidence 24/7 and, as soon as you can accept this, life gets much easier. In life coaching we are always saying things like 'expect the best' and 'don't settle for less than you deserve', and certainly it's important to go beyond our self-limiting beliefs to reach our potential. However, as a result, some clients believe that they should be totally positive all the time, and then give themselves a hard time whenever they find themselves falling by the wayside in the face of difficult challenges. Loving yourself doesn't just mean appreciating and valuing your witty, gorgeous, clever, positive, seductive, charismatic and brilliant side. No, the real challenge comes when you are facing your disbelieving, negative, self-critical and fed-up self; now she really does take some loving!

Your life will take you through emotional highs and lows. *Everyone* experiences both ups and downs. The key to a fabulous life lies in your attitude; it's not *what* happens that matters but rather *how you react to what happens*. The purpose of your life is much more than the successful achievement of your next goal; it's not the goal in itself that matters but rather how much you can love and appreciate yourself on your journey towards your goal.

Self-acceptance

Let's get back to basics. When you love yourself you will attract love and appreciation, and when you criticise yourself you will attract disrespect and victimising behaviour. Well, that's easy enough to understand, isn't it? All we need then is love, lots and lots of self-love, to become a love magnet extraordinaire! It sounds so simple, and yet . . . Loving and accepting ourselves is probably the most difficult thing we ever have to learn to do. Clients sometimes worry that self-acceptance is a form of complacency, which will stop them moving forward and changing, but actually the opposite is true. It may be a paradox, but the reality is that it is only when we can accept ourselves *exactly as we are right now* that we can begin to change and develop. This is because every time we slip into the 'not good enough' syndrome, we start hassling and haranguing ourselves and fall straight into the arms of the negative, self-critical downward spiral that takes us into the depths of despair. Self-change can never happen when we are locked in self-blame; we can only move forward when we feel positive about ourselves.

Jemima, 34, single mother of two children, perfectly describes how self-criticism can stop our progress. She says, 'The idea of loving and respecting myself has always been hard for me to grasp. I got into life coaching because I knew I needed to work on my self-esteem, but it was hard going. After my husband left, my confidence really fell, and I didn't know which way to turn. I would spend hours thinking about all the ways I had not been good enough for him and I wondered if he might have stayed if I had been thinner or cleverer or something. This train of thought always made me feel even worse about myself, and I would torture myself like this every night when the children were in bed.

'Life coaching showed me how to break this cycle by exchanging my negative self-beliefs for positive ones and by helping me to recognise the voice of my inner critic. Although I didn't really believe that *I am a winner* or that *everything I do is a success*, Lynda got me to say this sort of thing to myself over and over again, and eventually I started to believe it myself. I realised that the voice in my head that kept telling me off and saying that I was no good was not worth listening to because it only hurt me even more (it sounded just like one of my teachers at primary school). So I stepped out of a maze of negative thoughts that didn't lead anywhere and into a clear space where I felt so much better about myself. It was a revelation. Now

I do positive affirmations all the time; they keep my energy on track and keep me feeling OK about myself, even on a bad day. I can let myself off when I make mistakes now, rather than punishing myself over and over again (which never helped me). It's like I have stepped into a kinder more supportive cycle which helps me to keep faith with myself even when things are not so good. I have become much more optimistic and light-hearted and I am beginning to feel like the real me.'

Recognising your inner critic

We are our own worst critics. Who needs enemies when we are so good at bringing ourselves down? If you recognise yourself here, just relax; you are in the majority. The voice of our inner critic will always find something to, well, criticise us about! In our youth we might condemn ourselves for our insecurities and lack of experience; then, when we are older, we look back at that beautiful shining girl that we were and think, why didn't I appreciate her, just as she was? Apply that same logic now. Why wait for a retrospective appreciation? Why not have it right now in this very moment?

We can hang ourselves on all sorts of hooks: we are no good, too fat, too lazy, and not beautiful, clever or talented enough; we don't do enough, and whatever we do is never good enough! Why do we treat ourselves in such a harsh way? We would never dream of speaking so roughly to anyone else, yet we hurt ourselves continually with our self-judgements and disapproval. And if you think that you don't do this, just hang on a moment. Stop reading, close your eyes and listen to your mind. Hear it go! It never stops its ceaseless chatter: thinking, observing and passing judgements. Begin to notice the way you talk to yourself. Pay attention to your mental processes and become aware of how your thoughts affect your feelings and your behaviour. Are you kind to yourself? Do you forgive your mistakes and encourage yourself when you need a lift? Are you optimistic or do you worry about the future? Can you hear a note of positivity and hope or does a voice of gloom and doom drag you down? How do you talk to yourself?

We all have an inner critic, and its voice is loud and strident. It says things like: 'Who are you to think that you are any good?' 'Why would you think you can be/do that?' 'You are no good.' 'It's all your fault.' 'You can't trust yourself.' 'You will never be perfect.' 'I hate you.' 'You are stupid/fat/thoughtless/ugly/unkind.' 'You don't deserve anything.' 'Who would love you?' . . . Yes, you have heard this voice many, many times, focusing on your perceived weaknesses, filling you with dread and self-doubt, and laughing at your dreams. This voice talks to you from your own collection of past criticisms – those that you have heard from others and have chosen to believe. You might also notice that it speaks in a tone that you recognise from your childhood. Whenever you listen to your inner critic and believe that what it says is true, you will stay low in confidence; you will hate yourself and be unable to make positive changes. And who needs a no-win situation like this? Not you! You are free to change any self-beliefs that are not working for you. Your real and true self is centred and balanced, and she knows that you are amazing. She knows that you can only ever reach your true potential when your mind is clear and positive and supporting. Your real self speaks with a true voice and she will always encourage you. Even if you blow it in some way, your real self will remind you that *you are bigger than your mistakes* and will show you a creative way to resolve the situation. The diagram and exercise below give some examples of the ways in which your inner critic and your real self might talk to you.

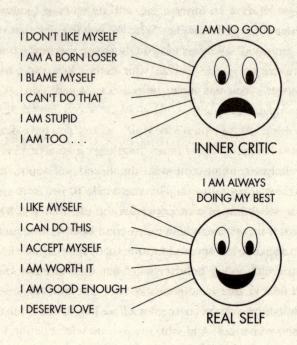

I AM NO GOOD

I DON'T LIKE MYSELF
I AM A BORN LOSER
I BLAME MYSELF
I CAN'T DO THAT
I AM STUPID
I AM TOO . . .

INNER CRITIC

I AM ALWAYS
DOING MY BEST

I LIKE MYSELF
I CAN DO THIS
I ACCEPT MYSELF
I AM WORTH IT
I AM GOOD ENOUGH
I DESERVE LOVE

REAL SELF

YOUR INNER VOICES

How are you talking to yourself?

Draw your own version of the Your Inner Voices diagram on page 252. Fill in the messages from your own critic. Remember this important point: you will never please this voice; its job is to criticise you *whatever you do*, and if you listen to it, you will always be a victim. Listen instead to your real self, whose messages transcend all others. Fill in the affirmations that your real self might be giving you, even if you can't hear them at the moment. Use the messages given in the diagram if you can't think of your own positive statements. Start saying these positive affirmations to yourself (act as if you believe them even if you don't yet) and slowly but surely you will let go of all those damaging self-critical beliefs. Stop beating yourself up, be at peace with yourself, accept who you are right now and know that you are always good enough just the way you are!

Are you loving someone else too much?

As we have seen throughout this book, self-belief and self-love create an aura of charisma and confidence that are very attractive. Love magnets draw others into their orbit. We know that two people who are high in self-confidence will bring their heightened awareness to the partnership, and there is a very good chance that they will enjoy a successful long-term relationship. On the other hand, a relationship between partners who are low in self-esteem and self-love is set for trouble.

Long experience of coaching and counselling has led

INSTANT TIP

LOVE AND APPRECIATE YOURSELF

As we have seen, it is all too easy to slip into negative self-talk, so here are a few ways to keep yourself in a positive frame of mind.

- Remind yourself of past successes.
- Know that your inner critic is always waiting to go into action; ignore it and its voice will fade away.
- Always ask your real self for an opinion; it will give you a realistic and creative response.
- Remember that you are not your mistakes. Learn from them, let go of them and decide not to make them again.
- The more you can love and appreciate yourself, the more others will reflect these feelings.
- Know that each time you recognise the voice of your inner critic and choose not to believe it, you will diminish its power over you.
- Surround yourself with positive affirmations (say them, sing them, write them down) and steep yourself in positive consciousness.
- Always remember that you are what you think you are, so think the best of yourself, always!

me to believe that there is a direct relationship between our lack of self-love and our attraction for men who are not good for us. And I can't possibly end this book without mentioning the work of Robin Norwood.

In 1985 Robin Norwood wrote a fabulous best-selling book called *Women Who Love Too Much*, which proposed the groundbreaking theory that most of us have loved too much at least once in our lives and that for some of us loving too much is a repeating theme. The concept of loving too much has now become a recognised syndrome in relationship psychology.

Women Who Love Too Much explores why women who are looking for love often find themselves in un-healthy relationships with unloving partners. Ms Norwood says that loving turns into loving too much when 'our partner is inappropriate, uncaring, or unavailable and yet we cannot give him up – in fact we want him, we need him even more.' Why would we let ourselves be treated so badly and why would we go back for more?

Both men and women suffer emotional pain; many women find this hard to believe because they have only ever had relationships with men who don't or can't show their feelings. Cultural and biological factors affect the ways that women and men deal with their hurt. As little girls we learn to use our natural female abilities (nurturing, sensitivity, receptiveness etc.) and we become very good at emotional caretaking. So when we are in emotional pain of any sort we try to cope by giving more and *loving more*. Men under emotional stress will cope in the ways they learned in boyhood – in a rational and conceptual way (avoiding emotions at all cost). Remember how under duress Martians choose to go alone to their caves while Venusians want to talk about their problems.

When their relationship hits stormy waters, men and women deal with their emotional pain in a different way:

Men cope by: looking outside the relationship and becoming absorbed in activities, **and women say:** 'Doesn't he even realise that we have a problem here? The more I need his emotional support, the more distant he becomes.'
Women cope by: looking at the relationship and trying to work out what is going on; looking at themselves and asking, 'What have I done wrong?'; thinking, 'What can I do to change this situation?'; trying to please their man; waiting for him to change. **Women say:** 'He really loves me; he's got so much potential; all he needs is my love, attention and help; I know just what he wants and if I can give him that then everything will be all right; I know he doesn't mean to be so thoughtless; I don't take any notice when he's like that – he's basically got a heart of gold; if only I can be patient enough to wait, I know that it will all come right in the end.'

Women who love too much need to be needed, and believe me there are plenty of men out there looking for a woman just like this. If you need to be needed, you will be looking for a needy man (and he will be looking for you). During a recent workshop of 30 women I asked how many of them had been in a relationship with a 'needy' man, and everyone put up their hand. We are often drawn to those men whom we see as being most needy – the exact form of neediness that attracts us depends precisely on our own unique blend of thought, feeling and behaviour patterns.

EXERCISE:

Your favourite 'needy' type of man*

The following are descriptions of types of men. Choose the ones that most attract you.

- Can't seem to settle
- Wild and irresponsible
- Addicted to something
- Ill
- Poor
- Depressed
- Stubborn
- Unable to communicate with others
- Unable to communicate with you
- Distant and remote
- Intellectual and preoccupied
- Abuses you
- Macho type
- Unable to commit himself
- Unhappy
- Sexually confused
- Needs your total attention
- Cold and unemotional
- Just needs *you*
- Has financial problems

- Is a workaholic
- Angry and temperamental
- Creative and depressed
- Confused 'new man'
- Unreliable
- Mean and moody

* Adapted from my book *Self-Esteem for Women*

Perhaps you are not attracted to any of these characteristics. So what 'type' of man do you fancy like mad, even if you know that he will be bad for you?

When we love and appreciate ourselves, we are high in self-esteem and we only become involved in nurturing, supporting and loving relationships. We do not need to be needed, so we do not attract a 'needy' man who requires rescuing. Our learned patterns of thinking, feeling and behaving are very deep. As we work on our personal development and confidence issues, we always need to be on the lookout for our self-invalidating and critical patterns (as expressed by our inner critic). If you find yourself being drawn into yet another caring role with a needy man, BEWARE! Stop and remind yourself of who you are and what you deserve. Women who love too much think that being in emotional pain is the same as in being in love. Remember that if it hurts, it isn't love! If it hurts, you are being victimised. Why would you want to be treated like this? If you are loving a man too much, you are loving yourself too little.

INSTANT TIP

REMEMBER THAT YOU ARE AMAZING

LEARN TO LOVE YOURSELF AND ALL ELSE WILL FOLLOW. IF THIS FEELS IMPOSSIBLE, THEN PRACTISE IT. PRACTISE BELIEVING THAT YOU ARE WONDERFUL, AMAZING, SIGNIFICANT AND DESERVING – BECAUSE YOU ARE! CREATE YOUR OWN LIST OF AFFIRMING SELF-BELIEFS. KEEP THOSE AFFIRMATIONS IN THE PRESENT TENSE, KEEP THEM POSITIVE AND PRACTISE SAYING THEM *ALL THE TIME*. SOME EXAMPLES MIGHT BE:

- I LOVE AND VALUE MYSELF.
- I AM FABULOUS.
- I AM A WONDERFUL PERSON.
- I DESERVE THE BEST IN LIFE.
- I AM UNIQUE.
- I BELIEVE IN MYSELF.
- I AM A WINNER.
- I AM AMAZING.

USE THESE EXAMPLES IF YOU WISH, AND CREATE SOME MORE OF YOUR OWN. LET THIS LIST BE YOUR FIRST RESOURCE WHENEVER YOU FEEL YOUR SELF-BELIEF WAVERING. SAY THESE THINGS TO YOURSELF AND THEY WILL LIFT YOUR ENERGY AND REMIND YOU OF YOUR INTRINSIC WORTHINESS.

Finding the balance

So how do you find the balance between loving someone and also loving yourself? Sometimes this can be quite a dilemma, can't it? He wants this, but you want the other. Should you stand up for your rights or compromise or let him have his way? When are you being a loving and supportive partner and when are you letting yourself be victimised? How much are you prepared to take before you will put your foot down? It's all a question of boundaries, and when you know where and what yours are you will be able to act appropriately.

Psychologically speaking, we refer to relationships as being healthy or unhealthy. It's easy to discriminate between the two: if your relationship is a healthy one, it allows you to satisfy your own basic needs. At times it might be difficult to recognise these needs; one effective way is to become aware of your own personal boundaries. Your boundaries are the limits you set. They reflect how far you are prepared to go in your relationship. Think of them as imaginary lines that you draw around yourself to stop others overstepping the limit (taking you too far). For example, a man could overstep your physical boundary by getting too close to you too quickly or he might invade your emotional boundary by being overly demanding or emotionally withdrawn (which is demanding in another way). When you are checking your boundaries, the question to ask yourself is: 'How far can I go with this person (physically and emotionally) and still feel comfortable?' When you are feeling uncomfortable in your relationship, you have let your boundaries be invaded. If this happens, stop and consider this carefully, then redraw your lines in the sand.

The following diagram represents a meeting between you and another person. Diagram (a) shows you and him when you first meet. Space lies between you both. Diagram (b) shows you coming together and interacting. You are sharing some space but your boundaries are

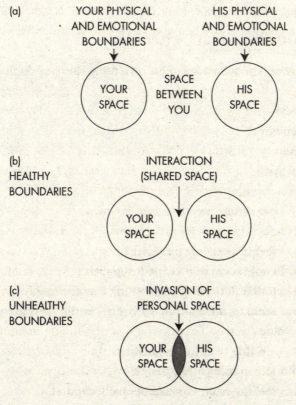

(a) YOUR PHYSICAL AND EMOTIONAL BOUNDARIES

HIS PHYSICAL AND EMOTIONAL BOUNDARIES

YOUR SPACE

SPACE BETWEEN YOU

HIS SPACE

(b) HEALTHY BOUNDARIES

INTERACTION (SHARED SPACE)

YOUR SPACE

HIS SPACE

(c) UNHEALTHY BOUNDARIES

INVASION OF PERSONAL SPACE

YOUR SPACE

HIS SPACE

HEALTHY AND UNHEALTHY BOUNDARIES

intact and you have a healthy relationship. Diagram (c) shows what happens when there is an invasion of boundaries. The personal limits of both of you have been blurred. Your boundaries and his have become inter-mixed. The relationship is unhealthy because neither of you has a true sense of self any more. Where do you end and where does he begin? Do you want to do this or are you doing it because he wants to? Look at the boundary checklist to see how healthy your own boundaries are.

Your boundary checklist

Answer the following questions, using these options:

Never
Sometimes
Often
Always

1   I put others' needs before my own.
2   I am good at making decisions.
3   I feel responsible for other people.
4   People seem to take me for granted.
5   I find it difficult to express my true feelings.
6   I seem to put a lot into my relationships and get very little back.
7   I am able to speak my mind.
8   I feel used by other people.
9   I feel the need to make people feel good.
10 I am victimised by other people.

11 I am frightened by angry feelings.

12 I make relationships with people who are no good for me.

13 I feel upset if other people are upset.

14 I am afraid to spend time alone.

15 Criticism really hurts me.

16 I stay in abusive relationships.

17 I trust myself.

18 I am very sensitive to the moods of others.

19 I find it difficult to keep a secret.

20 I can enjoy the success of others.

Think carefully about how each of your answers affects the quality of your relationships. Look in particular at the behaviour and feelings that you think create a problem in your interactions with other people; these are the areas where your boundaries are weak, and you will be feeling the effect in *all* your relationships. Wherever you have a boundary problem you will also have low self-esteem; poor relationships, unhealthy boundaries and low self-esteem go hand in hand.

E X E R C I S E :

Setting your boundaries

Step 1
Think about all your relationships and identify any ways in which people might be transgressing those imaginary lines that you have set in place to protect your needs. The key

question to ask yourself is: *does this person make me feel uncomfortable in any way?* If the answer is yes, how do they do this?

Step 2

In what particular situations do you need to strengthen your boundaries? Exactly how would others need to change their behaviour towards you?

Step 3

Communicate your needs to anyone who is invading your boundaries. Tell them what they are doing (for example, 'You are criticising me'). Ask them to stop doing it and warn them of the consequences if they don't ('Stop doing this or I will walk away'). And if they don't stop, you leave.

This isn't as hard as it sounds. Keeping your boundaries intact is just another way of taking care of yourself. Show your appreciation for others when they respect your boundaries and before you know it those around you will reflect your self-respect. As soon as you begin to love and value yourself, the people in your life will do this too.

The love of your life

Love is a feeling that lies within you ready to be awakened at any time that you open your heart to your life. When you are open-hearted you live your life with passion, commitment and enthusiasm; your true goal is to reach for your best and to appreciate and value every step of your journey. Your life becomes fascinating, and your energy and enthusiasm make you fascinating to others. Express your love for life and become a beacon of positivity; your enthusiasm will be catching and will draw other like-minded people towards you.

The love you feel for another depends entirely upon your capacity to tap into the love within you. A love magnet attracts others because she loves her life, she loves herself and she is a shining inspiration. Let your star shine, embrace your life and open your heart to love.

Love your life.

Love yourself.

Let your star shine.

MEDITATION MOMENT

LOVING WHAT IS

APPRECIATION IS THE KEY THAT OPENS OUR HEART. *LOVING WHAT IS* KEEPS US FOCUSED ON THE JOYS OF LIFE. LOVING WHAT IS MEANS STAYING IN THE MOMENT INSTEAD OF LOOKING BACK INTO THE PAST OR LOOKING TOWARDS THE FUTURE. THIS MEDITATION WILL HELP YOU TO RECOGNISE AND APPRECIATE THE MAGICAL MOMENTS OF EVERYDAY LIFE.

- Get comfortable and relax. Slow down your breathing and, if you wish, close your eyes.
- Concentrate on your physical body. Appreciate all the ways in which it works for you. You are a fabulous machine.
- Think of all the things you are good at. Pick them out one at a time and reflect on them. You are multi-talented.
- Become aware of the challenges you are facing right now. Give thanks for the inner strength and purpose you can call upon to help you overcome these obstacles. You have all the personal power you need.
- Think about your relationships with loved ones. Feel the opening sensation in your heart as you think about each one of them.
- Your life is a miracle; appreciate this.
- Love what is happening in your life right now, in this moment, and feel your heart expand. Yes, love is all you need.

Epilogue
Love to Love

Let no one who loves be called altogether unhappy. Even love unreturned has its rainbow.

J . M . B A R R I E

We love to love because it brings out the very best within us; we feel really and truly alive, and everything seems possible. The object of our affections gets all the glory for making us feel fabulous, but however gorgeous he is he cannot take all the credit. It's very important to remember that love lies within us, ready to be awakened at any time, and not necessarily by a handsome prince. Love is everywhere: in a selfless action, in a moment of appreciation and at any time we feel that it's just great to be alive.

Celebrate yourself and your amazing life and you will be filled with love and happiness. Spread these feelings around wherever you go, share your love and positivity and feel them magnify as they go out into the world and affect those who meet you. When you are loving your life, it will love you back in the most subtle and profound ways.

For those of you who are looking for love right now, just stop and look at yourself. Begin by appreciating what you have. In this way you will attract all you need. Be content with yourself and your positive feelings will shine through you, making you even more attractive to others. A great relationship with a fabulous man is entirely possible, but it can only materialise when you are high in self-respect and absolutely determined not to settle for anyone who is not right for you. Your first task is to work on yourself so that you have no need to look for a man to make you feel complete. Get your life in order and learn to be happy with yourself and you will discover something quite incredible: you have stopped looking for love.

If you are single, relish your independent status and recognise that you are a love magnet who is completely free to play the field and make her own relationship choices. And if you are in an unhappy relationship, it's time to face up to reality. Use the coaching techniques in this book to help you understand and change your situation.

Remember that you deserve a loving and supportive relationship and that this is your goal.

I have so enjoyed writing *Weekend Love Coach* and I do hope that it has been a support and inspiration to you. If you would like to get in touch with me or find out about my life coaching services just go to

www.weekendlifecoach.com

or email me at

lyndafield@weekendlifecoach.com

I look forward to hearing from you.
With all my best wishes

Lynda

References and Inspirational Books

Ban Breathnach, Sarah, *Romancing the Ordinary*, Simon and Schuster, 2004

De Angelis, Barbara, *Are You the One for Me?*, Thorsons, 1998

Fein, Ellen and Schneider, Sherrie, *The Rules*, Element, 2003

Field, Lynda, *Weekend Life Coach*, Vermilion, 2004

---- *The Self-Esteem Workbook*, Vermilion, 2001

---- *Just Do it Now*, Vermilion, 2001

---- *Be Yourself*, Vermilion, 2003

---- *60 Tips for Self-Esteem*, Vermilion, 2001

Gibran, Kahlil, *The Prophet*, Heinemann, 1970

Glass, Lillian, *Attracting Terrific People*, Thorsons, 1998

Gray, John, *Men Are From Mars, Women Are From Venus*, Thorsons, 1993

Greenwald, Rachel, *The Program*, Time Warner, 2004

Hay, Louise, *You Can Heal Your Life*, Eden Grove Editions, 1988

Hemmings, Jo, *The Dating Game*, New Holland, 2003

Heskell, Peta, *The Flirt Coach's Guide to Finding the Love You Want*, Element, 2003

Kamins, Marni and MacLeod, Janice, *The Break-up Repair Kit*, Conari Press, 2004

Lowndes, Leil, *How to Make Anyone Fall in Love with You*, Thorsons, 1997

McKenna, Paul and Willbourn, Hugh, *How to Mend a Broken Heart*, Bantam Press, 2003

Norwood, Robin, *Women Who Love Too Much*, Arrow, 1986

Pease, Allan and Barbara, *Why Men Don't Listen and Women Can't Read Maps*, Orion, 1999

Stanway, Andrew, *Intimate Solutions*, Vermilion, 2004

Weiner-Davis, Michele, *The Sex-Starved Marriage*, Simon and Schuster, 2004

Wiseman, Richard, *The Luck Factor*, Century, 2003

Vanzant, Iyanla, *Until Today*, Pocket Books, 2001

Index